D0202880

Robert Collie

Obsessive-Compulsive Disorder
A Guide for Family, Friends, and Pastors

More pre-publication
REVIEWS, COMMENTARIES, EVALUATIONS . . .

"Early in my ministry I made a home visit to a parishioner that astounded me. There was so much 'stuff' stacked throughout the home that only a path to the living room was available. I imagine most pastoral caregivers have encountered similar circumstances and have wondered, What is going on with this person? Doctor Collie not only provides insightful answers, but gives the pastoral caregiver technical assistance with proven methodology of care honed on experience. Whether OCD perpetuates itself in the form of hoarding, checking, straightening, or cleaning, it is clearly a neurological disorder.

As a worker in the field of alcohol and drugs, this book also offers insights to the relationship between OCD and substance abuse. However, possibly the greatest attribute of this work is the value to family and friends. For those associated with OCD family members, friends, or colleagues, this is a must-read book."

Barry Humble, MA
Executive Director,
Drug & Alcohol Consortium
of Allen County, Inc.;
Pastor, Boehmer United Methodist Church

"Dr. Collie has done his homework and has given the clergy a guide to helping those with OCD. Families will also find the book useful as it provides information to help them better understand the illness. As a result, the family can become a better support system for their OCD family member."

Jane B. Novak
Executive Assistant,
National Alliance for the Mentally Ill
(NAMI),
Fort Wayne, Indiana

The Haworth Pastoral Press®
An Imprint of The Haworth Press, Inc.
New York • London • Oxford

Obsessive-Compulsive Disorder

A Guide for Family, Friends, and Pastors

Obsessive-Compulsive Disorder
A Guide for Family, Friends, and Pastors

Robert Collie

The Haworth Pastoral Press®
An Imprint of The Haworth Press, Inc.
New York • London • Oxford

For more information on this book or to order, visit
http://www.haworthpress.com/store/product.asp?sku=5263

or call 1-800-HAWORTH (800-429-6784) in the United States and Canada
or (607) 722-5857 outside the United States and Canada

or contact orders@HaworthPress.com

Published by

The Haworth Pastoral Press®, an imprint of The Haworth Press, Inc., 10 Alice Street, Binghamton, NY 13904-1580.

PUBLISHER'S NOTE
Identities and circumstances of individuals discussed in this book have been changed to protect confidentiality.

Cover design by Jennifer M. Gaska.

Library of Congress Cataloging-in-Publication Data

Collie, Robert M.
    Obsessive-compulsive disorder : a guide for family, friends, and pastors / Robert Collie.
        p. cm.
    Includes bibliographical references and index.
    ISBN 0-7890-2536-1 (hard : alk. paper) — ISBN 0-7890-2537-X (soft : alk. paper)
    1. Obsessive-compulsive disorder—Patients—Pastoral counseling of. 2. Obsessive-compulsive disorder—Patients—Religious life. I. Title

BV4461.6.C64 2000
259'.425—dc22
                                                                            2004018860

CONTENTS

ABOUT THE AUTHOR

Robert Collie, ThD, is a pastoral counselor and a licensed clinical social worker with ChoiceMakers Counseling Service in Fort Wayne, Indiana. Dr. Collie is also a clinical member of the OC Foundation, a Diplomate of the American Association of Pastoral Counselors, and a professional consultant to an obsessive-compulsive disorders support group. Dr. Collie is author of *The Obsessive-Compulsive Disorder: Pastoral Care for the Road to Change* (Haworth) and *The Confessional Prayers of a Pastoral Counselor,* as well as a variety of articles on pastoral care and counseling issues. He is also a contributor to *The New Dictionary of Pastoral Studies.* Dr. Collie's professional interests include historical theology, innovative thinking on mental health, and pastoral counseling. His current research involves dual-diagnosis treatment of alcoholism and OCD.

Preface

Who This Book Is For

The idea of this book began in our OCD support group when one woman described how she had once gone to her associate pastor, overwhelmed by what she had begun to think and feel. Fortunately for her, she then went to the senior pastor. It was before we knew much about OCD, but he knew how to listen.

The book has grown out of ten years of weekly support group sessions. It is intended as a resource for caring persons wanting to be supportive of those suffering from OCD: pastors, pastoral counselors, chaplains, and a whole host of highly motivated social workers, psychiatric nurses, and marriage counselors. It is for all those persons whose work is both pastoral and therapeutic, a true priesthood of all believers who feel a call to care. I write from a Protestant Christian tradition, but I hope that others—rabbis, imams, priests—will translate the thoughts into their own traditions.

It would be the highest of compliments if a reader said to a friend with OCD, "Here's a book that I think you would like to read. Afterward, let's talk about it."

Coming to Understand Obsessive-Compulsive Disorder

As we caregivers consult, let it be said, "There is no 'us' and 'them.'"

The young mother was part of our support group, a half participant in our circle that meets in a church schoolroom. She had come several times, always toying with the idea of talking about her compulsion to clean. In a moment of long silence, one of the others leaned forward. "Are you having thoughts about killing your baby and you're really scared?" There was a torrent of tears; finally she realized that she was with family.

This was a reenactment of that ancient rite of healing, a symbolic laying on of hands.

In the ten years in which our support group has met weekly, this is not an unusual story. Ten years ago she probably would have been diagnosed with postpartum depression and never referred. Twenty-five years ago she would have been hospitalized.

Obsessive-compulsive disorder (OCD) sounds so clinically sterile when described diagnostically:

Unwanted interjected thoughts that cannot be shaken and compulsive mental or behavioral rituals to seek relief from those thoughts, the two of these taking up more than an hour a day; and significant interference in family, relationships, and work (including school).

When dramatized, however, it can make for good scripts. We saw that in the poignancy of *As Good As It Gets* on the big screen and on the small screen in the entertaining Frasier and Niles Crane characters on *Frasier* and in the bizarre antics of the detective on *Monk*. Note that in *Monk* he goes to the psychiatrist; in *Frasier* they are the psychiatrists! None of these shows, not even the weirdest TV documentary, does justice to the complexity of OCD, the mental health category with the greatest variety of religious expressions.

There was a time when some pastors knew about OCD, but not just any pastor. He would have been a Catholic parish priest. And he would not have known about OCD really, only about scrupulosity, "seeing sin where there is no sin." Today some pastors are cut off from this traditional knowing, ignorant of the whole issue. A very few might think OCD is demonic. Even to this day, an older person with OCD may come to a support group and share that an exorcism was tried on him or her!

In earlier years, the psychiatrists were not much better. Older support group members may recall how electric shock therapy was tried on them. As late as the *Diagnostic and Statistical Man-*

ual of Mental Disorders, Third Edition (and we are only at the fourth), OCD was listed as "a rare psychiatric condition." We know now that most sufferers simply refrained from discussing their obsessions and compulsions for fear they would be put in the locked ward.

The mental health scene was enlightened about twenty-five years ago when some researchers in the National Institute of Mental Health decided not to rely on the reports of psychiatrists and took their clipboards and went knocking on doors. Instead of a "rare psychiatric condition," they uncovered the fourth largest mental health problem in America. Now we recognize that this condition exists worldwide and overlaps numerous other conditions.

If you will allow me to share how I came to form and be the consultant to an OCD group, I would be glad to hear how you became one of those who care. It was 1972 when I saw my first case of OCD (of which I was aware). The counselee was a sophomore in college and shared her anguish about compulsively washing her hands. I had read about Freud's "Rat Man," and I tried my best psychoanalytical moves on her. That was not helping, so I tried what I had just been reading in family therapy. I followed that with a couple of West Coast techniques from Esalen lore; she gave up on me before I floundered further.

Going further back, when I was in graduate school I read *Young Man Luther,* by Erik Erikson. Erikson had much to say about "compulsions." It was fresh learning then. A couple of years ago when I reread it (now with years of experience working with persons with obsessions and compulsions), I was unable to relate positively to anything he had to say about them. What is known today about OCD would be alien to him; the knowledge explosion has brought us so far in only a few decades.

To be aware of OCD a person must have "eyes that see, and ears that hear," as the Scriptures put it. One Sunday afternoon my wife (a clinical social worker, well aware of OCD) and I were coming out of the Toledo Museum of Art and walking back to our car. As we were opening doors, we glanced into the car parked next to us. The backseat was packed high with newspapers and old fast-food wrappers, every kind of this and that other than a bailing machine.

The passenger seat was somewhat better, so the driver may have brought someone to the exhibit. Annelie and I looked at each other: we knew this was a hoarder. We hurt for the person: loving art on the one hand and yet having this particular neurological disorder on the other. We could well imagine the person's enjoyment of the exhibit and at the same time imagine what his or her home looked like. Perhaps you know of a similar situation. It is one thing, however, to wish to make it better; it is another thing to be able to help. That makes for a topic worth reading and praying about. By the end of this book, we will be exploring what you may want to do to help.

A reader may very well ask how anyone accumulates enough nerve to write about such a subject. As Joseph Ciarrocchi wrote in *The Doubting Disease,* to write about religion and OCD is to enter a trap—but it must be attempted. The interpretations of the dynamics of OCD and religion are my own responsibility. I can only plead, along with the prophet Isaiah, "Come, let us reason together."

In some sense, to write this book is similar to Mark Twain asking an older river pilot how he managed to learn all the sandbars in the Mississippi: "I've been on every one of them." Not true, of course, but applicable. More applicable, fellow pilgrim, is the rabbinical story of the man trying to find his way out of the forest who came to his rabbi for help. "I do not know the way out," said the rabbi, "but I have gone further into the forest than you, so come with me and we will find the way out together."

Acknowledgments

I would like to express my appreciation, first of all, to Robert Leslie, PhD. Dr. Leslie taught pastoral counseling both at the Pacific School of Religion and the Graduate Theological Union in Berkeley, California. From him I learned to value the work of small groups. A much greater lesson was learned by being his teaching assistant; he is a fine Christian gentleman in every sense of the word.

A deep sense of the privilege that I feel because of our association also needs to be expressed to those who have taught me about obsessive-compulsive disorder, the kind and generous persons who have participated these past ten years in our Fort Wayne OCD support group. Not even those who came and went in a single night have failed to be my teachers; many have stayed for many nights, and I thank them.

I would also like to express my admiration for two exceptional women. When my wife and I began going to the OC national conventions, they always led a support group demonstration. One of them, Patricia Perkins-Doyle, is now well-known as the executive director of the Obsessive-Compulsive Foundation. The other leader was Susan Duffy, whose inspirational work is less well-known to outsiders, but her knowledge, sincerity in being helpful, and comments in those early conventions are still valued by many.

I would be remiss if I did not thank the pastors and their families with whom I have counseled. A number of them had OCD, and it was with them that I first became interested in this disorder. Pastors are a courageous lot, among other fine qualities. I once did research on the incidence of OCD among the clergy in the North Indiana Conference of the United Methodist Church, and they responded beyond any researcher's reasonable expectations. A former counselee annually sends me a letter during Pastor Appreciation Week, and I am honored to be included in that number.

A variety of persons contributed to the manuscript, not all of whom should be named, for obvious reasons. Among those who can be, however, are clinical pastoral educator and supervisor John Peterson of the Lutheran Hospital, and the Fort Wayne Transactional Analysis Study Group. I have particularly valued the group's profound interest in religious aspects of issues, including mental health. A person in our OCD support group collected the stories appearing in the last chapter. Another group member read the manuscript and commented on it not only from the perspective of a person with OCD but also as a participant in the Stephens Ministry of her church.

I also want to acknowledge the contribution made by Prevesh Rustagi, MD, to my understanding of OCD. For a number of years now, Dr. Rustagi has been my psychiatrist consultant. I particularly appreciate the insights that he brings from a broader cultural perspective. Hopefully this book has value beyond the American scene.

Of course, there is Annelie, my colleague, friend, and wife, who discusses the conferences and seminars on the way home and reads proofs. As Dr. Rustagi has come at OCD from the perspective of one part of our globe, so Annelie has looked at it as a European.

Any of you should be so lucky to know these people! As the psalmist sang, "My cup runneth over."

Chapter 1

A Walk Around the Perimeter of OCD

THE NEED FOR BOTH PSYCHOLOGICAL INSIGHT AND SPIRITUAL DISCERNMENT

One of the elder statesmen of our support group is fond of saying, "Your God is too small." Perhaps it marks being one of the formerly scrupulous: he stole his saying right out of a book title by J. B. Phillips and isn't a bit sorry. In the course of confronting obsessive-compulsive disorder (OCD), one may or may not discover that a person's understanding of God is too small. It is a certainty, however, that a person's unexamined religious assumptions will be called into question.

Nice woman: she was kind and gentle, reared in a deeply pietistic way. She loved her bright red muscle car; she had always dreamed of having one. When she drove her other car into the garage, she parked it three feet away to keep from scratching it. She suspected the neighbors chuckled seeing her do it. Actually they must have scratched their heads wondering why she never drove it. She was terrified that if she did, her treasure would get dirt on it. So she just polished and polished. She confided to the support group that she wondered why, when she prayed about the problem, her prayer seemed to then get mixed up with the problem.

He loved his church, made every service when he wasn't working, and was a deeply dedicated tither. He confided his problem to the group at his first meeting: sometimes he would spend all night cleaning his kitchen floor. It was only after a long time that he admitted that he loved to play an instrument and had always wanted to buy a really good one, but he had never felt worthy.

For those who feel called to the ministry of caring pastorally, there is a need to be especially astute in our understanding of this condition we call obsessive-compulsive disorder. We begin to realize that the more we understand about it, the more we understand about ourselves as humans. In exploring the reality of the anxiety it reveals, we discover our need to accept the biological realities of our existence and our need to both set limits and challenge inhibitions. Although it is true that we are engaged in a study focused on the interplay of science, psychotherapy/psychology, and religion, the stage is set for us to discover the wonder in the opening line of Genesis: "In the beginning . . ."

Every faith group struggles with these realities. From my perspective, all caregivers will find their understanding greatly deepened and expanded by recalling the Apostle Paul's quest for freedom from the Law through faith in Christ—without neglecting the Apostle James' balancing of purity and good works. This is the perspective of the book, but many perspectives are brought to this world-spanning disorder. One of our group occasionally quotes from the Book of Mormon and neither attendees of Mass nor the most fundamental of Protestants are strangers there—and the "couldn't care less about religion" are always welcome. Let the dialogue begin: in community we sit around a big table.

WE DRAW FROM BOTH THE OLD AND THE NEW

Those in pastoral care may draw on old teachings, of course. In the Gospel According to Matthew (Ch. 23), Jesus pointed out how religious legalists could tithe even down to the most trifling garden herbs, all the while forgetting justice and mercy and neglecting the poor. This subdivision of OCD, called *scrupulosity,* is of especial interest to us.

If a person has OCD, it raises some interesting questions for pastoral care. According to the translators, Jesus said (but nowhere except Matthew 5:48), "You must be perfect, as your heavenly Father is perfect." Since those suffering from OCD are characteristically tormented perfectionists, how then is OCD a "disorder"? Recognizing the problems associated with trying to be "perfect," anyone knowing OCD can appreciate how Jesus reacted to one of his questioners. The man began, "Good Master . . ." Jesus scarcely let him finish, "Why do you call me 'good'? There is none good but God" (Mark 10:17 and Luke 18:18).

In our quest for understanding, it is wise to keep in mind that we are walking on a long—and broad—avenue of church history. Ignatius of Loyola, who founded the Society of Jesus (the Jesuits), feared to step on straws fallen in the shape of a cross on the roadway but out of his struggles rose to write an early pastoral manual. A young monk, Martin Luther, entertained the vain hope that he could relieve his waves of guilt by being allowed to confess and receive the sacraments several times a day, but he finally affirmed "the just shall live by faith alone." John Bunyan, as a youth, feared the steeple of the church would fall on him for his manifold sins as a child and was tortured by "the doubting disease" as soon as he began to believe he was saved, but went on to author *Pilgrim's Progress.* C. S. Lewis, author of *The Screwtape Letters,* fought with sadistic thoughts.

As we explore this "disorder," doubtless many readers will exclaim, "Oh, that reminds me of . . ." In the pages that follow, we are fortunate to have friends willing to share their experiences, and it is as much neighborliness as courage for them to do this, for we are all pilgrims here.

Jim's OCD first blatantly exhibited itself when he was stressed out as a freshman in college. When Jim went to the women's dorm to pick up his date, he would panic as he stood in the lobby; soon the rituals began. First it was checking and then it was counting. The doubting disease had broken out, and with it came scrupulosity, in Jim's case— at age nineteen—the notion of going to hell at the whiff of something sexual. A wise priest helped with this sense of "seeing sin where there is no sin." In case of doubt, he assured Jim that the priest took the sin upon himself if there was any. This reassurance helped for a time. The next part of the story was six years later and included seeing a psychiatrist. The doctor silently smoked a pipe and stared at his notepad; his soon self-terminated patient suffered for the next forty years without being able to give a name to what tormented him. In spite of needing to check and recheck, he continued to work, and worked well. He may have repeatedly feared he had hit someone with his car, but he never missed driving to an appointment: "I had a family to feed."

Now, as an experienced member of our support group, Jim often shares such stories with newcomers, adding, "and now I live a pretty normal life. Exposure and responsive blocking does it: bite the bullet."

This is not a particularly unusual story for an older sufferer; until recently it took an average of seventeen years for someone with OCD to get a clinically valid diagnosis. Now the average is dropping; hopefully a year from now, thanks to readers of books such as this, it will have dropped even further.

In part, why we—and the general public—have not recognized more persons as having OCD is that most information comes from television. On the one hand, each program has done the public an enormous service in publicizing this disorder; the problem is, of course, that every program has to compete for ratings, each trying to outdo the others. Two years after our group started, one of the members had an opportunity to go on a national television talk show. It would have been a brave coming out, for she had successfully hidden her compulsions. There was a long telephone interview; she never made it. Her suspicion was that she was no longer strange enough; once she had been but had gotten much better. She was disappointed in not being able to witness the before and after of effective treatment; had they known, there would have been a lot of viewers disappointed, too.

RETOOLING OUR THINKING

It takes "eyes that see and ears that hear" to recognize when and how a person is suffering from OCD; it was that way for a counselee one day. He came in, sat down, and started to laugh. On the way to the office he passed a man who had pulled over and was walking around his car, peering underneath. The counselee said, "I know what he was doing!" Maybe it takes one to know one, for he, too, had often feared the sound of hitting a pothole was really a body jolting his wheels.

When I was a young pastor, one family (very, very large) was there literally every time the church door opened. It was nice—although strange—how scrupulous they were about being in church, although I did not know the term then. The parents were always friendly but did not want me to visit. Once I insisted: I got only quick glimpses at the one room in which we sat. It was bare beyond starkness. I assumed they were poor—rightly—and might be embarrassed at the revelation of their poverty if the pastor came to call. I suspect now, after having been in some homes of those with OCD, that the room's bleak look signified that a cleaner and straightener was in charge; I simply did not know at the time what I was seeing. I also remember once being in the beautiful parsonage of a remarkably talented pastor and his remarkably at-her-prettiest wife; the home had a surgical look, it was so spotless. I thought it peculiar. I also recall once being in the study of a master of the pulpit; it was stacked with pile after pile of books, newspapers, magazines, and I-know-not-what in every chair but his. I had no idea what I was seeing; I supposed it was collected for his sermons. Only now would I have realized he suffered from hoarding.

Thus, working with OCD is one way for a person in a ministry of pastoral caring to sharpen his or her thinking. Take, for instance, a phrase used by a modern theologian to describe the Church: the Responsible Society. Sufferers from OCD are responsible, *overly responsible* being a characteristic of the disorder. The differentiation is helpful; someone with OCD may assume a fantastic responsibility for the welfare of another—whether the other wants it or not. It may be done to prevent harm from befalling a loved one, but tapping one's fingers in a rhythmic pattern is an annoying way of expressing care. In contrast, a member of the Responsible Society is apt to create a support group for those suffering from overresponsibility—and also to help sufferers stop magical thinking. Since OCD sufferers tend to be religious, it is important to challenge overt interplays of superstition and religion; in fact, a seemingly secular ritual such as counting often points to background religious issues.

For those in pastoral care, fascinating questions arise: For the mother who revealed her fear that she was going to cause the death of her baby, what is "badness"? For the parents who always had the entire tribe sitting straight and lined up in the pew, what is "goodness"? As we explore OCD, the valuing of "good" and "bad" persists, and is to be cherished rather than avoided. Frequently OCD is trapped in black-and-white thinking in a way that challenges our psychological insights. To be in pastoral care has an additional challenge: to learn spiritual discernment so that we may especially confront the superstitions that are so well camouflaged within run-of-the-mill religious thinking.

Because many sufferers with OCD have obsessions with violence (like the young mother), they always have an audit going on in their heads; those in pastoral care need to be competent in helping them resolve the dilemmas of columns of emotional figures that really don't add up. Central to this challenge is to know when to call in the psychiatrist as a matter of legal accountability and how to take advantage of the pastoral skills of "a physician of the soul." Most often it will require the particular abilities of many, for we are exploring a psychic black hole that sucks energy into it— one not in outer space but in the brain; a black hole sucking in both certitude and self-confidence that so disrupts the best efforts of pastor and parent, physician and priest.

It may be something of a puzzle that this disorder is preeminent among mental disorders in being expressed in religious guise. Even when the thought of having committed "the unforgivable sin" is a psychotic symptom, it is nevertheless an obsession. We will begin clarifying this in a later chapter as we explore the circuits of the brain in relationship to OCD.

There is another explanation to explore as well: obsessions often appear as unconsciously self-designated—actually explicitly contradicting the person's most precious values (such as a loving young mother, notable for her kindness and gentleness, who after the outbreak of OCD may obsess that she will harm her newborn). Probably nearly everyone has occasional mental belches we could characterize as "blasphemous"—ordinarily something verbal such as taking the Lord's name in vain rather than the behavioral variety more common in OCD—but only a genuinely religious person is upset by blasphemy. The secularist shrugs it off. Only the believer can curse—the unbeliever can do no better than get mad and cuss.

If obsessions ordinarily contradict the sufferer's most precious values, it would explain why persons with OCD so seldom strike others as neurotic—unless that disorder is combined with other mental conditions. There is not only an authenticity about their feelings but also a genuineness about their values, however biology has turned them upside down, from which no amount of psychoanalysis has been able to filter out a transference.

SCRUPULOSITY IS A SPECIAL CONCERN IN RELIGION

The issue of scrupulosity raises an interesting challenge to us in pastoral care. We rightly pursue those with a deficient conscience—"What does it matter if I take home this or that belonging to the company? They won't miss it"—but we neglect the overwrought conscience that trembles through a long night, reconsidering over and over if he or she misspoke a word and devastated someone's emotional life. Functional pastoral care confronts us with developing a balance of caring—to the tender hearted equally with the hard hearted—that has been neglected to the detriment of the whole community. It also raises issues of social concern.

One evening in Wiesbaden, we were having dinner in our hotel when a young couple came in. They must have just come from the airport. He was in his thirties, dressed in an expensive suit, as if the price of a Mideastern barrel of oil had gone up. Her swanky tennis shoes were the only nonscrupulous thing about the darkly garbed woman humbly walking the culturally prescribed two steps behind. As they ate, even her fluttery hand gestures were submissive. The next morning at breakfast, he was sitting with a gorgeous woman in a thousand-dollar outfit and they were looking into the soulful regions of each other's eyes. Her hands fluttered, but they did not strike us as submissive. Scrupulosity raises many issues, for the socially concerned; scrupulosity often carries a religious sanction.

Another factor to consider is that sensations of guilt are so frequent that having OCD is similar to having your own live-in IRS agent; many would agree that some moral or ethical audit goes on much of the time. Most persons in pastoral care can sympathize with such an ongoing audit. Fortunate indeed that they can testify that the feeling of such an audit moderates as a person matures in grace. What makes OCD especially fascinating, however, is that it is a partial audit: we will see how the perfectionist will strain to catch moral "minnows," while too frequently swallowing ethical "whales." On one hand, the audit is painstaking to the point of being beyond fussy, yet on the other hand, there is a continuum in which it can escalate into self-righteousness and then on into highly inappropriate aggressiveness.

These dynamics are in peoples, climes, and conditions. As a part of a travel group, we once made stops in Israel. Most of the group was Jewish, taking an opportunity to vacation and also to stop for a brief visit with friends and family. It was the Sabbath when we were in Jerusalem. We went to the Temple Wall and began to take pictures. An older man in highly Orthodox garb rushed up, yelling and grabbing at our cameras; it was an aggressive expression of scrupulosity. Photographing on the Sabbath violated his scruples; to the several people doing the photographing, it frustrated what would have been a precious religious memory. The Israeli guide was infuriated; that happens frequently with scrupulosity.

It should be remembered that we are dealing with a process. For example, scrupulosity has a "ground level," classically, the guilt-plagued scrupulous worrier at Mass; at a higher pitch of anxiety, the individual might be seen aggressively thrusting evangelistic pamphlets in the faces of passersby; finally, scrupulosity reaches a peak as a threat to a way of life, so that the disorder becomes a social contagion. Individuals may not be personally scrupulous, or act as if paranoid, but behave that way in public under certain circumstances. The worst case scenario is that the scruples associated with tradition become sacred and some "true believers" become violent when these are violated. It is as if they were obedient to the voice of God as they live out customs "of men," but more of this later.

ONE OF THE MANY PASTORAL CONCERNS IN OCD: LEAVE NO MOTHER BEHIND

As to the issue of OCD erupting in some mothers soon after giving birth, we do not know if this is as common as postpartum depression—or if the two are somehow related. For those charged with a ministry of pastoral care there is a lot to learn; what is not in question is that we represent a Lord who came so that persons weighted down by anxiety and guilt might have a higher quality of life and have it more abundantly. Where once the pastor laid his hands on the baby and blessed it, secure in the thought that the child would be saved, now we see that it may be the new mother who is in need of being saved.

This new mother, as others with OCD, needs to learn to differentiate the pathology of, "this is my OCD" and to affirm, "and this is me." We will be studying the passageway that leads back and forth between her "Real Me" and "Not Me" that gives birth to OCD. In this splitting of awareness, inevitably we will learn about ourselves as well, for we are searching the depths of what it means to be human rather than symptomatic. In doing this, we who care take our place in the thousand-year line of those pondering the mystery and majesty of Free Will.

QUESTIONS OFTEN ASKED

What causes OCD?

We don't know; when the standard explanation of "a chemical imbalance" is offered, it explains little but does affirm that the cause is neither emotional nor spiritual. Usually what was a trickle of unusual quirks, given enough stress, will burst through like waters over the spillway of a dam after a heavy rain.

For some women, giving birth and the accompanying hormonal changes will result in postpartum depression; for others, it is the beginning of suffering with fantasies of harming and of OCD.

We know that the stress factor for some with OCD was a childhood case of high fever, usually associated with a strep infection.

We do know that about one-fourth of the time, the genetic origin is clear; someone in the family tree will recognizably exhibit it. However, in most cases of OCD there is no history of mental instability or poor family background. Often there are no bad childhoods that would offer an explanation. No circumstances seem to foreordain OCD, although they may shape the form of the compulsions. This does not mean we cannot know; money is needed now for some very promising research projects.

Although we do not know causes, we know doctors can stumble into provoking OCD; an overdose of certain psychotropic medications may surface it—and then it will go away when the dosage is corrected. We know researchers can trigger it, so it can be studied: take an enormously brave person with contamination fears, wipe the restroom floor with a towel, put the hero into a brain scanning machine, pitch the person the dirty towel to hold, and *voilà!* The brain becomes livid with glucose consumption, signifying the activation of OCD. For anyone who thinks OCD is caused by dark, mysterious forces, one could say—in black humor—that this research is devilishly clever; the reality is that having learned how to get the disorder to kick in, perhaps now we can learn how to make it butt out.

How many persons suffer from OCD?

The general consensus is that about 2.5 percent of the world population will suffer from OCD at the clinically significant level at some point in their lives. From Paris, France, to Paris, Texas, straighteners straighten and cleaners clean. Compulsions that comfort do vary: in Zurich she may straighten; in India he may pull his big toe; for a Korean symmetry is soothing; and no one beats a Muslim for clean. Danes go for exhibiting scruples, but Muslims are reported to be hospitalized by them. Some Americans with OCD may prefer flipping an electrical switch, a very long shower, or hoarding CDs, but we are an equal-opportunity lot; you name it, and some of us will come up with an illustration of it.

When does it usually start?

The average age when OCD erupts in males is the late teens; in women, the early twenties. It has been reported as early as six months of age and is equally rare in the sixties. Almost all adults with OCD seem to recognize that there was foreshadowing earlier in their lives. We do know that the earlier the outbreak, the greater the odds that a close relative has it.

Do more men suffer from OCD than women?

No, the chances of suffering from it are equal. Some gender differences may be seen in rituals—more women may be cleaners than men, but not necessarily. Once I had to practically promise a wife I would not overtreat her husband so that she would allow him to come to counseling—his primary ritual was cleaning the kitchen for fifteen minutes when he came in from work!

OCD is free from prejudices. It will afflict an atheist just as readily as the most devout; it is totally color-blind, an unwelcome guest of both the rich and the poor, violating both the noble and the ignoble. Its only discrimination is that it seems, on average, to gift the sufferer with somewhat higher intelligence; perhaps the heightened struggle for the control of chaotic sensations has a compensating process.

What course does OCD usually take?

OCD fluctuates, ordinarily with the rising and lowering of stress levels in the person's life. This actually gives some control over it; if too hungry, too tired, too lonely, too sleep deprived, the person vulnerable to OCD can expect to have an increase of symptoms. OCD rarely goes into total remission, but some will have extended periods of relief, while others have only a brief respite. It may be the unique opportunity of pastoral caregivers to discover meditative means from our religious tradition to expand upon this relief.

Will OCD get worse over time?

Rarely; although it usually foretells its presence in some ways prior to full manifestation, once it develops, it stays pretty much at the same level. Its symptoms may vary—particularly if it begins early in life—but often OCD stays its chronic course. Sometimes its intensity lowers, however, as the person ages. This may be because the older person produces less glucose; perhaps there is a statute of limitations on how much some housewives are finally willing to scrub. It certainly means that combat with OCD produces veterans who become more accepting that for every wax there is a wane. For young people, death may be a frightening obsession; for those who are older, as one veteran pastor shared helpfully with a sufferer, "What's the big deal?"

Is OCD a serious mental illness?

It is listed as such psychiatrically, and unquestionably at clinical-level intensity it can necessitate hospitalization. Occasionally, some persons become completely dysfunctional. There are several good inpatient programs across the nation; in the worst instances, psychosurgery is considered. Sufferers are protected by federal law, just like others with medical disabilities.

It is fascinating that almost all of us have traces of obsessing and compulsion; but why not? Who does not have anxiety, and who has not found some routine for "taking the edge off"? Equally interesting is that having OCD does not mean per se that the person is neurotic, has a character or mood disorder, or is psychotic. The negative side is that OCD can be meshed with all sorts of other conditions such as phobias and generalized anxiety. Accurate diagnosis is a challenge because of the bizarre nature of some obsessions and compulsions, numbers of sufferers drink, and alcohol becomes the presenting problem; with others, it is more acceptable to be depressed than to risk being really crazy.

How has OCD been treated?

Poorly! At least in bygone days, but that is true of most early attempts at treating just about everything. Priests attempted exorcisms and physicians used ill-advised electroshock, and occasionally someone who suffered from these attempts may appear in support groups. Respectable therapists attempted cures by hypnosis, and psychoanalysts scribbled on pads and theorized in vain; less balanced patients have tried a lot of other things that are less respectable.

And today?

For a multidimensional problem, today a multidimensional answer is to be hoped for: cognitive techniques to strengthen and clear the mind; behavioral techniques to retrain the nonverbal responses of the more animal-like recesses of the brain. If necessary, a medication program is prescribed to help bring the intensity of physical responses down to a level where the mind may exercise its will to win. Several excellent medications are now available in the selective serotonin reuptake inhibitor family. After confirmation of a diagnosis of OCD, the standard operating procedure is to initiate an exposure/response homework assignment. Thirty days is the present consensus period for assessing the ability to accomplish homework assignments before beginning medication.*

Today a list of support groups and names of clinical members is available so that a referral can confidently be made (see Appendix A).

Is there any cure for OCD?

Seemingly not, if you are looking for absolutes. Asking that question is similar to asking if we humans can ultimately escape anxiety. We can moderate disquiet and unease, and we can control nervousness to some extent—but humans will never cease having

---

*The Expert Consensus Guidelines Series, "Treatment of Obsessive-Compulsive Disorder," John S. March, Allen Frances, Daniel Carpenter, and David A. Kahn, editors, *Journal of Clinical Psychiatry,* 58 (Supplement 4), 1997.

anxiety. OCD is physiological—and everyone has physiological problems, with or without OCD. Everyone has to learn how to manage life with blood pressure that is too high or too low, fallen arches, arthritis, vulnerabilities by the score. There are no exceptions to biology's erratic ways; supermodels may artfully pose for magazines, but super bodies are for too-good-to-be-true advertisements.

It is the person's values that seem to give structure to many of the symptoms of OCD, but we humans are not about to give up values, whatever trouble they entail. Although it is true that we humans are masterful worriers, it is equally true that there is a long pastoral history guiding our sense of values and modifying our deepest worrying.

Is there any hope for me as an OCD sufferer?

The Reverend Charles Dodgson, writing under the pen name of Lewis Carroll, was himself tortured by OCD. In *Through the Looking Glass* he addressed this question of hope by citing a poem familiar to all of us.

> Humpty Dumpty sat on a wall,
> Humpty Dumpty had a great fall,
> And all the King's horses,
> And all the King's men,
> Couldn't put Humpty Dumpty
> In his place again.

It is impossible to go back, but we are about to see that it is possible to go forward.

As a caregiver, you can answer, *yes.* But it will require two things for successfully modifying it: the physical courage to resist the brain's insistence that there is a terrible crisis, and the moral courage to live with less than certainty. Some will also state that courage arises from reliance on a Power greater than myself. Going it alone won't do it.

SUMMARY

We may conclude that suffering from OCD is living with extremes; in contrast, let us affirm that those we would describe as saintly cultivate a lifestyle that we may describe as having simplicity. A beautiful Shaker folk hymn affirms this:

'Tis a gift to be simple,
'Tis a gift to be free

and with this comes peace. The extremes of OCD are a denial of this style. The hoarder attempts to find peace in having; the cleaner and straightener moves beyond simplicity by attempting to find peace in barrenness. In the pastoral way, peace comes not as a cure, but as a healing. And it is, indeed, a gift to be simple— but ironically, an Amish teenager's hands redden as readily as an agnostic's. The sufferer would escape suffering if he or she could; the mutual task of giving and receiving care is to work one's way out of a dead-end canyon and into a life more abundant.

Chapter 2

Getting to Know OCD

HELPFUL TERMS

Anxiety

Anxiety is the heightened sense of alertness necessary for survival, a constant readiness to fight, flee, or hide; fear and worry are ordinarily more concretely focused. In English, "anxiety" is a generalized condition, the trade-off of having a higher form of thought, and catastrophizing is the downside of foresight. OCD is unlike phobias; in a phobia we are dealing with the fallout of an actual experience. In OCD we are attempting to cope with a neurological condition that results in a biological predisposition.

In this disorder, the symptoms often enact a scenario for survival—the washing, the checking, the fear of damnation—and the body's chemicals are always ready for aggressive behavior or panicky flight. When the alarm bells of insecurity go off, they usually signal the mind and total body to speed up—it is as if the brain is yelling to itself, "Think fast!" In OCD this anxiety ordinarily takes the form of hypervigilance so that the body tends to go quickly into emergency mode. The different consequences of this vulnerability are intertwined: commanded to "think fast" (but not to be impulsive), overanalysis takes place. Too many options are seen, doubt churns, and possibilities multiply.

In a rarer form of OCD—slowness—the survival tactic is to hide; at this extreme, everything tends to shut down, and sufferers play possum. While some sufferers' thoughts may feel speeded up, a few experience themselves as in slow motion. A good schoolteacher, upon reading this, may wonder how all this relates to ADD (attention deficit disorder, sometimes with, sometimes without, hyperactivity).

For our pastoral thinking, we often use a different term than "anxiety": angst. It is a German word, largely identical to anxiety, but it carries a different connotation, heavier, more filled with dread, a sense of the alien. We all have anxiety, but not OCD-intensity anxiety, which is more loaded with impending doom. In English, anxiety carries more of a connotation of worry or nervousness; in German, angst is often called, *Lebensangst,* with the connotation of fear of life itself, a physical sensation of dread. It is as if anxiety is similar to an impersonal siren at a firehouse; the angst of OCD goes off like a burglar alarm. Only at times of lower stress will the person with clinical levels of OCD experience anxiety as if it were the wail of a far-off siren; even then it is almost always experienced like background static on an old tube radio.

Perhaps we who are without a clinical level of OCD can never truly experience what living with OCD means, this waiting for the next shoe to drop. It may, however, have similarities to the feelings of someone who has been though a tornado when TORNADO WARNING runs across the television screen, for OCD shares some traits with post-traumatic stress disorder. To get at *Lebensangst,* ask someone with OCD about the mass of sensations accompanying the thought or image that first sets off obsessing; it will be difficult for the person to communicate, but perhaps similar to a veteran describing what combat is like. One is the fog of war, the other the nonverbal sensations arising from the midbrain, the "fog of OCD" that we work to dissipate.

Intrusive Thoughts

"Intrusive thought" or "automatic thought" are phrases used in OCD literature to indicate an unwanted idea or image intruding into a person's awareness, much like a burp. In OCD the unwanted thought usually is of incest, contamination, violence, or blasphemy—not just unpleasant, but damned unwanted by those fearful of being damned. One might describe these sensations arising from the basal ganglia into consciousness as "the acid reflux of the brain."

This sensory faculty in the central part of the brain begins as a sensation of alarm before intruding upon consciousness: first it produces an unusual electrical "spike," then electrochemical messengers are sent through the body and induce a chemical response to the felt crisis. This includes an intrusion into the mind that results in a conscious thought interpreting the sensation (such as death or harm coming to a loved one). The sensation is, of course, prelogical, and a transition occurs between it and the thought arising from it, so there is never an explanation of the thought, only an explanation of the sensation. What can be expected then is that in the vain pursuit of an explanation, a superstition will often appear to create some sort of linkage of happenings.

For this reason, I use a more descriptive phrase; instead of "automatic thought," as in some OCD literature, I use the phrase "reflex thought"—a "knee-jerk interpretation." The reflex thought can have interpretive variants, for it is often not a purely cognitive event. Tunes can be heard that cannot be dismissed or visual distortions may be seen such as a dent in another car that was not even parked close.

If we regard the reflex thought as similar to post-traumatic stress, it opens up a number of healing possibilities. If we understand the impact of some past trauma splintering the person's present sense of reality, we may better grasp the impact of OCD. In this disorder, both past and present threats spiral together to rupture a person's sense of immediate reality by compromising his or her ability to will to be fully present.

Obsession

An obsession is an unpleasant thought that a person cannot shake; it may be, however, a persistent tune or an unshakeable question in a father's mind whether he has unwittingly committed incest with his young child. The emphasis is on *unwanted* and on endless repetition. The obsessive thought varies greatly with the individual, whether of saying a prayer *exactly right* or of fearing harm to oneself—or of harming.

The obsession sets off a mental process similar to a string of dominoes set up to tip each one over in turn, but it may be equally.

appropriate to designate an obsession as a fixation. We will see how both are valid perspectives when we discuss how the circuits of the brain function in this disorder. In the case of obsessive praying, a thin line differentiates it from a compulsion, so that "fixation" may be the more descriptive term; in this context, the title of Jeffrey Schwartz's excellent book, *Brain Lock,* is highly relevant.

An obsession, as process, might be also thought of as similar to ruminating; we can note a similarity to such a characteristic in serious depression, which could help explain why OCD and depression are often seen in combination. In all of this, we cannot help but be struck by the characteristic of experiencing an extreme: either fearing harm or doing harm, or blasphemy being part of the same disorder as a compulsion to pray. Not just any old praying: perfect praying.

Another way of looking at this process is in terms of an anxious person climbing a ladder; the reflex action arises when the climber looks down and sees how high he or she is. We might think of the obsession as freezing up on the ladder: he panics; he grips the ladder; his eyes clamp shut; he cannot move. That physical response is compelling in the extreme. Understandably, the person whose insides are shaking does not appreciate someone yelling up, "Oh, don't be silly. Just stop it, you ninny, and come down this very instant!" For those in pastoral care, it is important to realize their arrival has been preceded by a great deal of high-minded advice giving, probably followed by well-intended scolding. Unconditional positive regard is a prerequisite for pastoral care, but neither reassurance unlimited nor high-minded lectures are integral parts of effective treatment.

Understandably, a sufferer often will question his or her own sanity. One difference is that an obsession is a voice *heard within one's head;* if the person were psychotic, the person would be hearing the voice or voices coming from *outside* his or her head. The psychotic person often is characterized by hearing accusations; in OCD, the issue is more likely to be self-berating.

The obsession presents itself, in one sense, as an unending series of "yes, buts." It is annoying not merely because it cannot be shut out, but also because it constitutes a threat to the integrity of the person's identity, in either a moral, physical, or intellectual sense. "I am a logical person. I have locked the door; nevertheless I am hit with 'yes, but,' and so I check, even though it violates what I logically know." The next phrase understandably may be a series of put-downs about being weak, crazy, and so forth. "I'm Suspicious of Me" is the signature song when an obsession is blaring in concert.

Compulsions

A compulsion is a behavior that relieves the anxiety associated with the obsession. For example, a possible contact with germs leads to a fear of contamination and from there self-comforting through hand washing. The angst aroused by going to school or work may drive the person to seek temporary relief, perhaps through compulsively changing clothes. This feeling of being driven to placate apprehension takes different forms. Checking the locks on the windows before leaving home is but one of the many forms of what appears to be procrastination. The lateness characterizing some church members is caused by changing clothes several times: "Honey, I'm sorry. But I just can't make up my mind." But it is not about shoes. Relief through rituals is sought in strange packages, all with an early expiration date, all without logic.

Where do these rituals come from? No one knows; perhaps the vulnerability to angst is the constant, with primitive memories on some level of the unconscious giving shape to habit. The dynamic may arise from that developmental level in which the young child loves to demand, "Read it again, Daddy"—and Daddy had better not change a word of it. The heredity and environment of the individual's circumstances add another variable defining the formula through which relief might be taught. There is one certainty: there are never enough distractions to relieve one's inner state for long.

Rituals

Some rituals are so common to some times and places as to scarcely arouse notice, such as crossing oneself to forestall the evil eye or fingering worry beads. For this reason, the term *ritual* is at times used to describe a compulsion due to its similarity to religious rites. A person with contamination fears may take compulsive showers, each conducted in *exactly* the same sequence, as if some strange rite of purification was being held. For the person, it is as if time stands still; the reality is, of course, the compulsion lasts until the chemical spurt of anxiety in the brain has had time to be discharged. Then the person is released as if from a spell.

A person with an "undoing ritual" will have a "bad" thought (a reflex response to some trigger—some form of black cat has crossed his or her street) and then consciously attempt to rub it out with a "good" thought. It is much like the superstitious tossing salt over their shoulders. Reverend Cotton Mather of colonial New England developed a one-sentence prayer to counteract such bad thoughts.

These bad thoughts are overvalued until they have tremendous power, as if they had a voodoo-like magic. A PhD in science who has OCD could well have an overpowering sensation of having the accursed mind power to cause someone harm unless some undoing ritual was performed. Curiously, most frequently the person, however intelligent, initially will not have the insight to realize that these fears express a form of superstition. Not realizing this, the person launches a whole series of repetitive good thoughts to avoid doing harm, as if a white magic thought could counter a black magic thought. Many of us probably have unconsciously developed a "one liner" to help neutralize the acid reflux of some painful memory; it is all very preconscious.

In its purest form, a ritual or compulsion is philosophically neutral from a value perspective, like a child flipping a light switch to reduce anxiety. In philosophy it may be value neutral, but in vivo it is highly annoying. A ritual represents a functional value; for the sake of the family, the housewife with OCD is trying to ensure the clothes are free from contamination. If a clean towel falls from the washer to the floor, it gets washed again; the health of the family is at stake. The goal of the ritual, from a value perspective, is to restore the person's sense of the integrity of the self through the medium of a moral, mental, or physical purification rite: "I recheck and recheck this lock to be free from error so that our home will be safe." Unfortunately, OCD's giggle is always subliminal: "April Fool!" The ritual is dysfunctional because it is an extreme.

The Disorder

Although there is no need to define "disorder," it is fundamental to working with OCD to keep in mind its neurological basis; it is "disordering," or perhaps we can also say "disorienting." The person trapped in the shower loses the sense of time; the person shaking a door lock acts as if the ordinary process of memory has malfunctioned. Some sufferers have so much difficulty with dislocation that they will drive only the same route so as not to become lost. Judging distance is thorny; when driving, pedestrians walking along the sidewalk appear to be much closer than they actually are.

Sin

In working therapeutically, it is important to repeat that neither the obsession nor the compulsion is a sin, in and of itself; both are outbursts of chemically induced sensations from the midbrain. *Sin involves the full consent of the will.* It is always well to remember that a person with OCD is quite capable of feeling guilty about Lincoln's assassination! *Sin intends.*

Scrupulosity

A term frequently seen in OCD literature is "scrupulosity." It is rooted in the Latin term *scrupus* for a small sharp stone that gets into a shoe; in religion, classically it refers to "seeing sin where there is no sin." Probably the best illustration of contemporary scrupulosity, however, is Tom Friedman's column in *The New York Times* (October 19, 2001), "A Tweezers Defense Shield," after airport security impounded his tweezers soon after 9/11. Airport rules and regulators were confiscating tweezers and nail clippers—while letting passengers board with cigarette lighters.

Proverbially, the sufferer makes a mountain out of a molehill, and long are the tales in support groups about who can outdo the others in having to recheck all the groceries at home to make sure the store owner was not cheated by an item slipping by the cashier; no trip across the city is too long if the person at the checkout counter gave a dollar too much in change. An admirable quality when combined with common sense, in OCD this intensity of honesty expresses the disorder succinctly.

A second classical phrase also applies to scrupulosity: "the defective conscience." This refers to being overly focused, a vulnerability to the teeniest scruple in such a way that the scrupulous person is blinded to broader ethical implications. The great scriptural discussion of scrupulosity is, of course, Jesus' speech recorded in the twenty-third chapter of Matthew, decrying those religious legalists who would strain a bug from a cup but who would swallow a camel. Alas, perfectionism leads to such excesses that its ideals make hypocrisy inevitable. Anxiety has caused the person to be hypersensitive to some value, exclusively focusing on it—yet demonstrating a spiritual blindness in a more significant area. For instance, in yesteryear some pious church member could refuse to go to a picture show but turn a deaf ear to racial slurs.

Perhaps a key to scrupulosity is to think of it as a side effect of idealism. This idealism can also become externalized in an aggressive way, as when some preacher makes hospital visitations so belligerently that the patients become upset. In the classical religious literature on scrupulosity, this form is categorized as "collegial." We will use a more direct phrase: "aggressive scrupulosity." Few muggings leave deeper bruises than being mauled by a moralist acting on a matter of principle.

Avoidance

Avoidance is the attempt to escape from a situation that predictably sets off the OCD alarm system. Just as a person with agoraphobia will avoid open spaces, the person with contamination fears may avoid public restrooms; a person with contamination fears concerning disinfectants may feel driven to avoid the aisle in the grocery store where these products are shelved. It is important to know what triggers these frights and to differentiate that from the root cause of anxiety. Once the sufferer recognizes that OCD casts a spell similar to a primeval taboo, then avoidances can be faced in a more determined fashion.

Inhibition

Slightly different from avoidance are certain inhibitions, such as not being able to go through a doorway. The eighteenth-century genius Samuel Johnson would have to twist and literally hurl himself through one. In a more modern inhibition, with which some will identify, the sufferer has great difficulty in writing a check. Fifteen minutes is not too much time to take to perfect the writing of the monthly electrical bill. It takes another five minutes to work through being irresolute about dropping the envelope into a mailbox. It is another example of paralysis by analysis. Here again we see a continuum: inhibitions at one point, avoidances at another, and phobias usually close by.

Overvalued Ideas and Magical Thinking

We need terms to describe types of thinking when discussing OCD. If a person drives ten miles after leaving work and suddenly realizes he did not turn on the security system in the office, the thought is not unrealistic, nor is turning around and going back. If a person is hit by the reflex thought of an office fire erupting because she did not turn off the electric pencil sharpener, that is an overvalued idea. If the person starts tapping on the seat in sets of five to prevent a fire, this is described as magical thinking. In OCD, this is not a psychotic process but an example of superstition.

Triggers

The vulnerability to the extremes of insecurity may be set off in several ways. First, outside physical influences may trigger OCD, such as a car hitting a pothole driven by a person with that "flavor" of OCD. Second, internal influences may operate, as in a shift in the balance of hormones after the birth of a baby. Attacks may also be triggered by symbols such as seeing the word *witch*. The numeral 13 may send emotional vibrations spinning through the body of some sufferers. This more accurately describes the "gating" in the neurological loop. Finally, an accumulation of stress may lower the guardrails of attention to the present and allow dark sensations to undermine consciousness: too lonely, too hungry, too sleepy, too tired. Coping with OCD in some ways demands the self-discipline of a diabetic with his or her diet.

Codependency

Another term to consider is "codependent." Originally it came from the field of alcoholism: on Monday mornings the wife called in for her alcoholic husband to say he had the flu. In the world of OCD, as elsewhere, it indicates being a collaborator with pathology. Many a codependent parent or spouse, as well as a pastor, has been trapped into offering reassurances to those in pain caused by a tiny but extremely sharp-edged scruple. More likely, enough failed attempts and finally a parent resorts to corporal punishment or a pastor avoids the parishioner.

TERMS MOST USED IN THERAPY TODAY

A frequent term in the treatment of OCD is "behavioral therapy"; an associated term is "exposure/response," although the latter word is actually better referred to as "response (the compulsion or ritual) blocking." The treatment is similar to working with a person having a phobia concerning heights, with the treatment objective being the ability to get up on a stepladder. What is sought is not to get a job as a high construction steel worker but to be able to clean the gutters. The process is gradual. It could involve, for example, getting out the stepladder (exposure) and not running off to go shopping or watch TV (response blocking) until the chemical urgency in the brain has run its course. The counselee who goes up and down enough times will achieve *satiation*. The process is straightforward; repeat it until the counselee is unutterably bored instead of anxious. The therapist prescribes homework assignments to achieve this, such as in the case of a person with OCD who fears he or she has run over someone every time there is a bump, by prescribing a daily drive for two weeks over a dirt road.

Desensitization: if the ruts don't do it, the dust will! But take it a "baby step" at a time.

However, it needs to be noted that a purely behavioral approach leaves much to be desired. In contemporary therapy with OCD, it is usual for cognitive approaches to be combined with behavioral approaches. The cognitive treatment deals with the obsessions; a behavioral component most often addresses the compulsions. When medication is added, it is in support of the cognitive-behavior treatment plan, not as a substitute.*

A number of technical terms are used to describe therapeutic techniques, such as habituation and satiation, but at the risk of being simplistic, what they boil down to is similar to bringing up a baby. At an appropriate time, the baby should be ready to sleep all night—a time of great rejoicing for parents. The baby, however, has learned that if he or she cries, instant comfort is available; expertly applied squalling gets results. It tears out the mother's heart to hear her baby cry; she jumps up and brings comfort, which is all too temporary. The cognitive part of therapy is for the new mother to talk to her mother. The advice is to let the baby cry herself or himself to sleep; it won't hurt the baby, but this is easier said than done, as most parents will remember. For the sake of everyone, however, the baby is allowed to cry; a lot of squalling results and a few tantrums. The mother's jaw has to clinch (and she must distinguish when the baby really is sick and needs help) and tough it out—and gradually the baby does sleep all night. That is the essence of cognitive-behavioral therapy. It works, too.

The Spectrum of OCD Disorders

Relatively rare disorders such as trichotillomania (hair pulling), kleptomania (compulsive stealing), Tourette's syndrome, and hypochondriasis (obsessions with illness) sometimes are brought to the attention of a caring person. These are discussed in Appendix C.

---

*To flesh out these definitions, three generic OCD stories are given in Appendix B.

SUMMARY

The sheer variety of forms OCD takes is bewildering, but remember: an advantage of pastoral care is that family members are more often included in the talks than if the sufferer is simply seen in individual psychotherapy. In a support group the meeting should always be inclusive, "open" as they would designate it in AA. Husbands do speak up; wives will confide. Many times the pastoral caregiver knows the whole family and has a grasp on the work situation, places, circumstances, and relationships. The pastoral office does not have to be occupied by a person who is healthy, wealthy, or wise—in the ways of the world—but does require an openness to seeing the whole picture.

It is an awesome responsibility to be a caregiver; not least that the caregiver goes to those with the doubting disease with a great many reservations as part of the pastoral baggage. Caregiver and care receiver are equally human. There is one great learning experience about which each will agree. We know intimately what the Apostle Paul shared with the Christians at Rome: "The just shall live by faith alone." The leap of faith is a decision, and fear and trembling come fully assembled and require no batteries.

If we can be more comfortable in the presence of questions and quietly share the living out both of our faith and doubts, our carers' experiences may become care receivers' lurch toward faith. When the irresolvable questions plague us, such as "Why? Why, O Lord?" we can only fall in with the long line of pastoral caregivers who have not flinched in doing their duty, even in darkest night.

For those who have OCD, it takes physical courage to bite the bullet and face the task; but it takes moral courage for us to go to them and empathetically enter into the experience and support their efforts. It is important to create a feeling of togetherness, rather than mere encouragement. It is in community that the spiritual is discovered.

Chapter 3

Putting the Pieces of OCD Together

HELPFUL GENERALIZATIONS

As this guide is offered for continuing education discussions by caring groups, as well as for individual readers, the topics will be indicated by numerals for easier identification.

1. *Obsessions and compulsions invariably contain a kernel of truth.* A person with contamination fears may overreact to lawn sprays as if they were instruments of mass destruction—but they do have their downside. It is proverbial that "cleanliness is next to godliness," and cleaning is not always excessive; it has been said, "a penny saved is a penny earned," and the hoarder is not always completely mistaken; a checker may become frantic with the need to check, but a wise parent teaches the child to stop, look, and listen. With this kernel of truth, the problem comes—as the Apostle Paul might phrase it—when the Law is hardened into legalisms and principles stretch into scrupulosity.

2. *The next generalization has to do with intensity. The disorder of thinking obsessively and/or acting compulsively is that of exaggeration, so that a virtue grows into a vice.* For example, to use the rearview mirror when driving is good sense—to stare constantly into it is OCD. It is a religious obligation to witness to one's faith, but to act out in the compulsion known as collegial scrupulosity is to be aggressive. When we speak clinically of OCD as an anxiety disorder, it is not an off-handed comment: not "overly anxious" but "hyperanxious," just as we might speak of hyperthyroidism. This hyper-response in an automatic one. The resultant angst has a magician's ability to delude the brain into perceiving a crisis. Con-

tamination fears can reach such an intensity that the sufferer can feel the door handle crawling with germs. It is a partial truth but there is an inability to adequately identify and resist the exaggeration. The partial truth becomes a "brain lock," and the pastoral goal of becoming open minded is not a cliché.

OCD can even include the condition known in psychiatry as "derealization": a person may glance into a mirror, see herself, and, with dismay, experience the false impression that what she has seen is not real. Fortunately, it is rare; unfortunately, we know it is a trick but we do not know how OCD does it.

3. *The disorderliness of OCD involves a continuum.* Hoarding ranges from thriftiness to miserliness, and on to the house as landfill, where the public health people need to step in. Trichotillomania ranges from a bored teenager twirling her hair to a compulsive hair puller who must wear a wig. Symmetry spans the length from a harmonious dinner setting to a husband who literally cannot tolerate the stress if his wife moves his meticulous desk arrangement when she dusts. The intuitive sensing of placement that leads to the waves of upset has to be believed, but it almost exceeds belief unless personally experienced.

4. *A key general notion to ponder about OCD is that it somehow combines both uniformity and diversity to an unusual degree.* Across the world, the ritual of symmetry brings comfort, and rites of purification produce calm. The range of rituals is astonishing: from the head rocking of the autistic to the methods of a mental giant like Samuel Johnson, who lured sleep by calculating the width of the road if the national debt of Great Britain were in silver and were used to pave a highway around the equator. OCD is a prime example of globalization, as it is so universal. It may take unique forms, such as a person picking at his toenails instead of the usual fingernails. It may also take a musical form, such as a tune that persists until the person fingers out the notes on the piano, or that keeps sounding for months in the person's head in spite of anything and everything. In studying this disorder, we are reminded that we all are of the same order: human, both uniform and highly individuated.

5. *Frequently a quality of superstitiousness is present.* Persons with OCD have an unwelcome sense of imposed, unwanted mind

power: think a bad thought and it will actually harm someone; instead of having the mind-power to do something like bending a spoon, the sufferer may live in fear of hurting other people.

A second aspect of this is that the person with OCD has a stronger than normal desire to anticipate the future so it can be controlled. One genuinely religious sufferer had the fear that his strange compulsions were related to the black magic practices banned in the Old Testament. As a matter of fact, when fighting OCD it is well to associate the rituals that attempt to know and control the future with reading tea leaves or the lines on a person's palms: the gypsy fortune teller in us all becomes larger than life in OCD.

6. *OCD is an exaggeration of the normal.* Compulsive hand washing is a prolongation beyond what is desirable. To vacuum and be unable to leave a line showing is not a desirable display of perfection. With eight hours of nighttime cleaning of the kitchen, few would debate the diagnosis.

We might regard OCD as an inappropriate mixture of primitive anxiety and the values learned as we have been socialized. In regard to scrupulosity, for instance, we might consider the quip that "becoming a PhD is knowing more and more about less and less!" Thus scrupulosity is based on law, a written language, and scholarship: combine that with primitive anxiety and we have a frightened overanalysis of what is good. Exaggerate what is desirable and behold: a vice.

7. *We need to keep in mind that the psychiatrist does not become professionally concerned until disordering thoughts and repetitive behaviors total over an hour per day and create havoc with relationships on the job, in the school, or in the home.* It is in this context that those in pastoral care become concerned, but as a quality-of-life issue rather than a psychiatric one. These generalizations become guidelines to help us explore some of the mysteries of human behavior, as when an otherwise normal teenager refuses to get a driver's license; the psychiatric and pastoral inevitably do overlap, as when a person so fears a fire may start at home that she takes all the portable electrical household items with her to work. The psychiatrist can but medicate her anxiety; it is the pastoral caregiver who addresses her superstition.

SEEING THE PROCESS LAID OUT

We are now in a position to be clear about the sequence of the process in OCD:

1. The sufferer is vulnerable to a molten cauldron of anxiety, biologically prone to excessive insecurity.

2. When these sensations belch into consciousness as a reflex thought, it is as if that thought is borne along like a rock on a meltingly hot flow of sensations.

3. The person begins to double *and* redouble this thought into a scenario of "what ifs" that we call the doubting disease.

4. At some point the chemicals are exhausted, the attack is over, until the person becomes sufficiently insecure once again. Repeated attacks cause deepening despair.

5. Relief will again be sought by mental or behavioral repetitions to mute or numb the feelings until this cycling has run its course. Unfortunately, repetition wears a rut in the roadway of a looping circuit in the brain.

THE NECESSITY FOR A HOLISTIC APPROACH

Biologically, when most severe, OCD is regarded as a medical condition and for that reason is covered by federal disability legislation.

In OCD, we are exploring a multidimensional process necessitating a holistic understanding. In the therapeutic, the parts are intriguing, but it is the whole that must be grasped, such as when a sufferer sitting in a chair is talking calmly to a friend, all the while secretly and superstitiously tapping her fingers in patterns of three to keep her husband safe from harm.

This disorder is a neurological condition in which the symptoms are frequently expressed in terms of human survival. It follows, therefore, that the spiritual can no more be excluded than logic or emotions in coping with this problem. In the example of the tapping fingers, the woman may need medication to ameliorate the intensity of her feelings, but the fact that she associates the pattern of threes with Father, Son, and Holy Ghost may be a complication. She will need to disentangle some religious notions as she confronts superstition with logic and finds ways to moderate her emotions.

Likewise, no simple explanation can be made to the college student about why he is so fearful unless he touches each door frame before he goes through it. He may even suffer so intensely that he has taken on OCD as a part of who he is. Consequently, a religious concept, such as becoming "a new being in Christ," is highly relevant to the whole of his healing.

AT THE EXTREMES: AN EMPHASIS SOLELY ON A PHYSICAL OR MENTAL POLE

Hoarding is part of a continuum, for it exists in many degrees and forms. In financial matters, it ranges from the thrifty to the miserly. It runs the gamut from the person coming home from work and spending an hour with his stamp collection, to the person hoarding thousands of Internet files, to the person handicapped by an inability to throw anything away. In this terribly severe form, the person cannot throw away the accumulating piles of junk mail or the daily newspaper (or even goes in search of junk to collect) to the point where only trails exist through the landfill the person calls home. With the physical pole exploding with collecting, the mental pole is so blocked that activities such as bill paying or locating vital papers become impossible chores.

Neurologically, it appears that the activity of the brain in hoarding is found much to the rear of the forebrain. If this should prove to be true, it would explain why categorizing is so difficult, why evaluating is so thorny, and even why it is true for some persons that when things are put in drawers, they are out of sight, out of mind. We know of neighbors in every community who suffer in this way and whose family life, too, becomes a mess.

For those who care, in extreme cases, often the first step is to insist the person unblock the windows and doors to make an escape route in case of fire; sometimes the person, if living alone and older, can be motivated to clear areas to prevent falling and breaking a hip. In some circumstances, the inheritors of the estate just hope an arsonist will take pity on them so they will not have to clean it out; almost universally, there is family disruption as a consequence of this neurological condition.

Many children of hoarders simply refuse to go home again, believing they are dealing with a parent's kooky choices, ignorant of the reality of quirky biology. Good intentions sometimes worsen the situation: the adult children may sneak into the home when the hoarding parent is on vacation and, thinking it would be an expression of love, scour it. Hell hath no anguish like the robbed nest of the hoard, a sanctuary has been desecrated, a self-identity despoiled.

The pastoral task is to seek a consensual acknowledgment that the condition is neurological, and therefore morally and ethically neutral, however much it may provoke the public health department, thus setting the tone for the reconciliation of a family divided. The next step is to call in the "expert," which, unfortunately, is still very much in the research and development stage.

At times it seems possible to identify what gave shape to hoarding: a child traumatized by a family burned out with the loss of everything or a farm situation where every part of the pig was used except the squeal. What makes hoarding so tenacious is its primordial nature. It has the appearance of being grounded in a sense of incompleteness, as if the serpent was whispering to Eve in the Garden of Eden, "just add this and keep that and you will demonstrate a godlike wisdom, prepared for anything and everything." Articles may be saved by the stack with a vague notion of getting around to them soon, or things may be warehoused to be sufficient against whatever want someday might bring.

At the opposite end of the OCD span, in the pain of scrupulosity we see the saying illustrated, "too good for his (or her) own good." The person is moral, ethical, and above and beyond conscientious: responsible to the uttermost. There is a drivenness toward flawlessness more often than of the love of God. There is no length to which the person will not go to be utterly correct. He or she will be more Catholic than the pope, having rectitude rather than relationships. Although scrupulosity would appear to be good, it is necessary to remember, however, that the virtue of goodness is impossible to sculpt out of fear: correctness, yes; goodness, no. There is a great deal of the positive in having scruples, for who in a world of those who would kick a golf ball on the sly to improve a lie cannot love those with scruples? Scrupulosity, however, is a good born out of time and place, a wobbly half step beyond oneself in human development.

SUMMARY

Those who care, then, deal with the issue of deepening spirituality as well as the need for pastoral care of those tortured by feelings of being damned for what is at best dubious to the rest of us. The spiritual issue for the hoarder is less evident but terribly keen. The home of the hoarder may strike the lay observer as a packrat's nest, but spiritually it is a *sanctuary,* experienced much like a city of refuge in the Old Testament sense, to which the innocent can flee for safety. The question is, "But who pursues? And from what?" The conflict frequently associated with the lives both of hoarders and those with extreme scruples is that of fleeing from a lion only to meet a bear.

For all those suffering with OCD, the concern to finally confront is: "On what does my security ultimately rely?" Shall I, like the hoarder in the parable in the gospel, gather my all into barns and refuse to think that sooner or just a bit later, my comfort zone shall stand an ultimate cross-examination? As to scruples, is not "correctness" a mechanical rabbit to chase, and the scrupulous the straining greyhound?

Chapter 4

How OCD Affects the Person

IMPLICATIONS FOR THE PERSONALITY OF THE INDIVIDUAL

In OCD support groups, someone will occasionally quip, "*normal* only exists on the dial of clothes dryers." In this instance, however, let us presume that normal means successfully evaluating the reality of a stimulus setting off an alarm. In therapy, denial is often worked through by therapists; with OCD, the need is to work through inflated ideas.

1. The assumption that best fits the obsessive-compulsive disorder is that it is grounded in the neurology of the individual; the best explanation would seem to be that this neurological condition results in a heated dialogue between two parts of the brain. The outcome for the personality of the person experiencing OCD is the consequence of being caught between the blare of an alarm going off and the persistent yet failed response of reason. *The person with clinical-level OCD lives with conflicting feelings, both physical and mental.* These conflicting feelings result in a condition of self-absorption. This condition ordinarily is not narcissistic—with its demand of being entitled to a special place in the sun and a tendency to believe others will enjoy one's flourishes—rather, it is a teeth-grinding frustration of being imprisoned by unwanted and unintended thoughts and needs.

2. A consequence for the personality is an inner push toward secrecy, for who would willingly be around anyone with a mind so polluted? OCD sufferers almost inevitably conclude that anyone feeling the thoughts—and at the same time realizing the contra-

dictions—must be crazy, and they are not about to share that with anybody.

3. What furthers the bewilderment is the awareness that, from a purely intellectual standpoint, OCD sufferers may have tested as superior to their friends. The problem, however, is that academic intelligence is different from emotional intelligence, and one cannot always make use of it.

4. No personality description, such as introvert or extrovert, matches one-to-one with OCD. Personality is an outward manifestation; OCD is debated inwardly. The observed behavior in OCD is similar to the tip of an iceberg; it is not so much introversion as it is that the sufferer finds it difficult to experience intimacy. The unseen of the person is simply too large.

5. There are characteristics of the OCD conflict for the pastoral caregiver to keep in mind when preparing to assist in the ceasefire negotiations of what is essentially a civil war. Persons with OCD are not mere worriers, although worriers and those with OCD are *both off balance because they live with one mental "foot" always anticipating* the next step; it is realistic black humor to observe that they live in the future tense. Jesus' sayings challenging sufferers to live one day at a time are very relevant when they are used as sharing, not sermonizing.

6. Because living with OCD is like waiting for the next shoe to drop, it is astonishing that some sufferers are able to be achievers: it is so natural to slide past setting goals. A compulsion brings comfort, but stalling (changing clothes several times, for instance) until the chemically announced crisis passes means that whatever was intended is frustrated, such as getting a child to school on time. Trapped in the bubble of the moment, it seems simpler to drift than to will. This gives us another factor to consider in effective treatment: sometimes identifying the most necessary, rather than the simplest, objective is necessary from a relational perspective.

7. It is a part of the conflict that those with OCD are resistant to change; change, whether positive or negative, brings stress, and stress increases anxiety. Again, there is a paradox: when confronted with an unavoidable challenge, such as a dying parent or the terrorism of 9/11, the demands of reality likely will surface a

calm acceptance (and often a steely adequacy to the challenge of the situation). If there is doubt in anyone's mind, watch and admire what happens to OCD when the sufferer is a parent and his or her child has a broken leg. When the floodwaters of genuine need arise, OCD gets swept away. Such observations are the pragmatic basis for the therapeutic technique of flooding. At ground level, Reality is friendly.

8. The checking, straightening, and cleaning may not be soon moderated, but by the grace of God, the malicious self-condemnation of this child of God is under an order to cease and desist by a Higher Court. It is true, of course, that the sufferer would quit if he or she could. There is a balance in the scale of things, and this balance at times can be tipped. This is an area in which the pastoral caregiver exercises the authority of Scripture in full: the Word of God going up against the dictates of the flesh. The mutilation of the mind, just as much as skin picking, is at stake.

9. The uppermost question is *the degree to which this individual is vulnerable to angst*. With successful treatment, the person may then give the lock one shake (or two) to be sure the door is locked and then go off to school with the carpool, perhaps physically shaky, but not shaken in conviction. Probably no one with OCD ever gets to the point where he or she can speak contemptuously of a mere chemical reaction, but they no longer allow themselves to be fooled by it. They know they can often outfox it by simply outwaiting it. The body is designed to flush out wastes—Biology 101, Theology 101.

10. In Ignatius of Loyola's phrase, *these are people with a "too-tender conscience"*; they fill the mourner's bench, while the hardhearted are more apt to be found sitting and smoking on the steps of the church. A person with OCD afflicted with an obscene reflex thought will not fall willingly into the category of what others shrug off as locker-room talk. If the obscene is being indulged in as entertainment, the person is not experiencing OCD.

11. Understandably, *the sufferer with OCD has low self-esteem*— "If others are so secure in their faith, why aren't I?" They try to fight off doubt as if it were a sneak thief; they attempt to stop their ritualistic behavior, but nothing works quickly enough, and the stomping on self-identity by self-condemnation begins: "weak,"

"stupid," "crazy." In the beginning of healing stands the prohibition against judging oneself.

12. Another observation must be made here, for OCD does not solely consist of "tying up the person's life in knots." Often there is a painful level of inhibitions, as in the woman who loves to bake but cannot make a birthday cake for her favorite nephew for fear she might unwittingly poison him. Every day is April Fool's Day with OCD; it is an impractical joker preventing a parent from doing needed routines. Part of the freedom to which we aspire in pastoral care is freedom *to* and not merely *from;* it is the *freedom to* that often makes a difference in where to begin when a treatment program is thought through.

IMPLICATIONS FOR RELATIONSHIPS

Sufferers with OCD tend to be very nice persons. If they get themselves in trouble, it is likely to be by needing to please; they are among the last persons in the world to want to hurt anyone's feelings, much less their bodies. They most frequently suffer from a form of OCD that demands a constant perfecting of behavior. Consequently, they will apologize beyond all measure to make certain they said or did the right thing. The untoward word is apt to produce a sleepless night: the need to be liked almost always wins. One night at ten o'clock, the parish priest was astonished by a knock at the door. Charles Darwin, the famed biologist, had not said *exactly* what he wanted to say at a committee meeting that Sunday afternoon.

1. *Persons with OCD do need to be certain,* however, and if a person with OCD irritates others, it is likely because he or she is grasping at a reassurance that evaporates even in the exchange. The need for certainty is frequently a cause of classroom conflict, as well as family conflict. If a fourth grader is a level-ten frustration in class because is he unable to stop asking if his friend really is living in Denver now, he has level-100 misery at bedtime.

On the religious level, the pathological need to be certain throws light on an area of theological controversy. It may not be common sense to deny that those committed to their faith cannot backslide, but in times of intense anxiety, many religious persons suffer enormously from their biological predisposition to doubt. The doctrine "once saved, always saved" then becomes something to be grabbed with both hands, life with a life back guarantee.

2. There is anger, but usually not hostility or passive aggressiveness, rather fury over the inability to do what needs to be done or prevented. For instance, the person with OCD can have road rage (just like anyone else), but it is important to understand that it is most often impersonal, directed at no one, especially the family. OCD is not an impulse-control disorder, much less a character disorder; it is rare, indeed, to find a sufferer who is undercontrolled, except at the furthest ends of the spectrum.

3. *Control needs mark the OCD dynamic* as the sufferer tries to fight off what is anguishing to him or her. Contamination fears may even lead the sufferer to try to force a spouse to change shoes and clothes several times after coming home. If having a phobia the person might avoid elevators; with OCD there is also a persistent effort to dodge what might trigger a threatening outburst, but often these triggers are less identifiable. Persons with OCD are often seen as controllers but do not experience themselves as wanting to control others; they are simply persons whose world is full of stimuli coaxing out their dread. They feel a need to cope with their environment, but their way of coping has unintended consequences.

Consider the strange but true stories such as that of a loving husband who insisted that all the knives be kept in the garage because of his fear of harming his wife. One such husband had no fear if either one of them was using an electric knife. In fact, he insisted he would not be bothered by using a chain saw as long as it was an electric one with a cord attached to it. The more obvious explanation is that the memory area of his innermost brain had nothing encoded in it having to do with electrical matters. Consequently, electrical items never caused a crisis response.

Persons in relationships with OCD sufferers nevertheless often feel controlled, for knives are needed for cooking. Spouses unwillingly learn to tiptoe around the eggshells of stressors—and eventually are themselves not slouches in regard to attempts at control.

In reality, they are both caught up in a peace-at-any-price dynamic, one inner, one outer. This is the result of more than normal nervous tensions rather than either being bad persons when the accusations begin to fly in marriage counseling sessions. Once stress is acknowledged as a key variable in an onslaught of OCD, controllable day-to-day pressures can then become the object of discussion rather than someone's flawed personality.

4. *There is a need for perfection* that ordinarily is not so much a desire as a fear of the consequences of going astray. It is OCD that whispers insistently, "Get it absolutely right and you will be safe." A well-run home may possibly be felt by some wife as marital job security—but imagine having to vacuum the rug in such a way that not a single line will show. Imagine what it is like to have to clean the telephone every time your husband uses it or the door handle if a friend of your child should inadvertently come over to play.

Understandably it puts a strain on relationships. Little gratitude is to be expected if the husband feels his health is only preserved by the wife's exactness in arranging objects on his chest of drawers. The husband is apt to find a direct way to express his opinion that this concern for his health illustrates a sense of overresponsibility; the wifely response is then apt to illustrate a need for reassurance also characteristic of the disorder. Each distances the other from intimacy. Now, as usual with OCD, there is a paradox to cleaning and straightening, for what began as a value resulted in a lack of intimacy, one value clashing with another. The question of what is most important is a vital issue in treatment.

5. Another area of conflict is that persons with OCD also are *sometimes seen as messy (lazy or procrastinating)*. These characteristics usually reflect inhibitions and frequently provoke judgmentalism in others. In the case of hoarding, however, the problem may be that the sufferer literally experiences "out of sight, out of mind." Out of sight in a drawer may actually mean to some hoarders that a thing has ceased to exist if it is out of sight. All the possible illusions and rationalizations do not matter to a son or daughter if papers are piled about and on the stove. The demand is to clean it up and throw it out. Unfortunately, "can" is not an operative word for a hoarder—but treatment techniques are becoming available.

Others fear to get started. With cleaning, for instance, they may be afraid that once started they will be unable to stop. The perfectionist has no shutoff valve marked "this is good enough." A worry-prone teenager may take several lengthy showers a day—seemingly concerned with cleanliness—but his room will have clothes piled several inches thick on the rug. If, and when, he starts to clean, however, it will be done with a meticulousness that is mind-boggling to the parent, and just as frustrating: "You don't have to do all that. Just pick it up and put it in the dirty clothes hamper." All this appears to be a quarrel between two parts of the brain trying to settle how much is good enough as if the issue is homeland security. Hopefully the teenager will pass beyond it, but anxiety may evolve into spreading angst.

It was in this context that one of our support group members shared a life-changing moment. She was driving home feeling the full force of despair and self-loathing when she happened to glance at a roadside church bulletin board. It read, "God Doesn't Make Any Trash." She told herself, "If God can love me, I can." It became the road next taken, a different loop in the circuitry of the brain began to glow with energy.

So it is that a hearty "atta-girl" or "atta-boy" is in order whether for limit setting or limit pushing: the person activating pastoral care is always a person demonstrating a feel-good about any accomplishment, a baby step at a time. Many individuals never learned as children to congratulate themselves, and the pastoral person becomes a teacher and role model. The "pastoral" of counseling is as often reparenting as it is reframing a faulty perception.

IMPLICATIONS FOR EFFECTIVE CARING FOR THE INDIVIDUAL

Pastoral caring is a mirroring of loving both yourself and your neighbor. Therapy begins as a reflection caught by the sufferer in this mirror. It results not in a revolutionary overthrow of the OCD, but in an evolutionary transformation.

Mere ordinary living, to use a basketball analogy, needs the ability to dribble well if ever a score is to be made. It is an interesting image, giving us a clue and a measurement for success in helping those with OCD: because daily pressures are inevitable in any person's life, we want to increase their—our!—ability to bounce back. When a person with OCD starts on the road to health, he or she is most apt to rebound about as easily as a flat basketball; in the process of becoming healthier, it is as if more "air" is being taken in, inner firmness becoming more equal to outer pressures. Mental health brings the ability to bounce back faster and faster, to utilize change, to respond to need and opportunity. It is the ability to improve the rebound time that marks the therapeutic response to pastoral care.

In terms of working with a relationship troubled by OCD, it is important to remember that the focus must be on the OCD. The individual is primary; the relationship is secondary. If the persons come together for support, it is the obligation of the person with OCD to work on OCD; the other person (who may well be an enabler to work on that issue) must intelligently support that. It is only after the OCD has been reasonably resolved that relationship issues become available for resolution.

SUMMARY

At times a person is tempted to smile at some *larger-than-life cascade of guilt* of those with OCD. One of my favorites (person, as well as illustration) was a postman suffering from scrupulosity, who was tormented about stealing dirt on his shoes when he walked across a lawn. It is only when the suffering is truly heard that any startle, for *any* strangeness, is banished. A trigger of anxiety acts as if it were under magnification; that characteristic must have served our species well in some fashion, or it would not have evolved and certainly would not be maintained. Unfortunately for persons with OCD, its ways and means have about the same degree of relevancy as a buggy whip.

When considering all that having OCD can do to a person, let us remember a treasured testimony from one of our support group members: "I finally realized that I could never be so perfect that God would love me."

Chapter 5

It All Starts with the Brain

WE ARE GETTING CLEAR PICTURES OF OUR BRAINS

If an adult experiencing the outbreak of OCD does not believe he or she is crazy, now that is a story that ought to be cheerfully shared, for how can a rational person know he has just put down the garage door, yet be overpowered by a dreadful uncertainty? In the litany of checking and rechecking, the next sound heard is not from the garage door but from spouses pulling out their hair in frustration. Or, to turn this in another direction, imagine the electrical graphing of the brain of a person suffering from OCD. Suddenly there is an electrical spike signifying there will be a transition from a feverous sensation, into an unwanted, perhaps hellish thought. But is that spike really going to affect the eternal destiny of the sufferer? It is difficult to believe that even one of the ancient gods monitors brain waves so seriously, yet many sufferers misconstrue this feverish distress as meaning they are being damned to hell. Intellectually they know better. Theologically it is ridiculous, *but*. It is the "but" with which persons in pastoral care work.

Little wonder that in previous years the quite rational sufferer was loath to see a psychiatrist and spill out what psychoanalysts would note as "overvalued ideas." The crazy-making contradictions not only violated the person's logic, they also appeared to make a travesty out of what many faithful persons believed to be true of the very heart of Reality. Treatment seemed a double bind: damned if you do and damned if you don't.

In OCD there is the body/brain/mind with its sensations/emotional/intellectual feelings, *but also* the spiritual—the ability to transcend ourselves and which respond to wider values. In pastorally caring, we work with the person in moving toward wholeness from the very beginning when we affirm as a basic premise that we are dealing with a neurological disorder, for this affirms that the condition has definable limits. To affirm OCD as biological in nature is not simplistic, materialistic, or disloyal to whatever credo is personally affirmed by the caregiver or care receiver. Excruciating OCD is; demonic it isn't: Biology 101, Theology 101. This affirmation of a neurological process forms the basis for moving toward wholeness.

Let us begin with the brain, a family of members. You can picture the outline of the brain in a textbook, but when you need to explain it to someone with OCD there never seems to be a textbook around. Certainly no one in pastoral care has a plastic brain sitting on the desk, but a little knowledge goes a long way.

For utilitarian learning purposes, make a fist (a "family of fingers") and turn it toward you. Use the outline of the brain you remember from a textbook as an overlay on your fist.* The back of your hand is the back of the brain; the nose is toward you.

Four fingers are tucked inside; the tips of the middle fingers represent the basal ganglia. This is located in the middle of the brain in front of the spinal cord. The alarm system is in this region, just as it is in the systems of other higher mammals. For humans it is also a center for producing a sense of dread.

If you will notice where the first joint is on your fingers, that represents the area associated with religious feelings.

Going up those two middle fingers, as you pass the joints, you enter the area of the orbital frontal cortex. Now we are in the region that we begin to associate with the mind. Here we are in that unique area of awareness in which we, of all the species, realize that we must die.

Imagine now that there are five loops, up to down, fanning out from the tips of your fingers from the first joint up to the knuckles. They are neurological circuits. You can imagine where the eyes are, and consequently how close the optical nerves are to the lowest circuit.

---

*The idea of using a fist is taken from *Phantoms in the Brain,* by the neurologist V. S. Ramachandran.

The lowest of these five neurological circuits, the loop related to OCD, is adjacent to the area associated with religious feelings. Now we have a notion why OCD and religious feelings so often run together. It also suggests why there are so many optical illusions in this particular disorder.

The reality of the loop itself is important for therapy. The loop begins in the basal ganglia, the source of anxiety. The stimulus travels up the excitatory side of the loop into the forebrain area, becoming a conscious thought. Then the stimulus returns along the route in which closure is made or where it can become modulated. The returning stimulus at this point should be "gated," unfortunately, with OCD the "gate" has been left open.

We might consider the implications of this fist simile for thinking about the OCD extremes of hoarding and scrupulosity. What both scrupulosity and hoarding have in common is the basal ganglia, an area associated with fearfulness; we might think of it in the palm. The difference is that the area of electrical activity in hoarding probably is from a more primitive area of the brain. Scrupulosity would have an area of stimulation toward the joints of the finger, for scruples have to be taught and that requires sophisticated language skills.

The idea of using a fist to discuss the brain may strike a person as far too gross. The reality is that ten years ago pictures were drawn of the brain showing specific regions related to some specific function; today this happens more rarely. The brain has fluidity. If there is a lesion on the left side—which ordinarily would support the developing of reading—the brain of a young child sometimes shifts that function over to the right side. The Creator may have taken off on the seventh day, but he didn't quit the job.

In the process of OCD, the triggering stimulus from one of our five senses enters the region of the brain where the alarm center is located, buried deep like a wartime command center. What happens next depends on the individual's vulnerability to angst. If someone is overly prone to being alarmed, the body's system for fight, flight, or hiding goes off too readily, triggering chemical messengers to rush everywhere. As if in wartime, an urgent signal drafts the Mind member of the brain community; glucose is rushed to the "front" and increased blood supplies can sometimes even be felt as the forehead warms. The resultant unspeakable dread we humans have fortunately learned to name and therefore to explore rationally is OCD.* As to the notion of going to hell for failing to turn off the office typewriter—this is not God, but the overresponse to what the brain puts off on the mind as an impending disaster.

If we humans were only more like animals, when the alarm system was set off, we would take a few jumps like a deer or rabbit and stop to do a reality check; we could then continue to high-tail it, go back to browsing, or freeze in the attempt to invisibly blend in. This is probably what would happen if we were dealing only with the basal ganglia. Our emergency alarm system would have an automatic shutoff, but therein lies the problem with OCD at the clinical level, for the system is prone to false alarms. A trade-off of moving beyond even the higher mammals into a newer cognitive level is that to some degree we have lost our "horse sense." The automatic shutoff system is out of kilter.

We can now see the direction of being helpful to sufferers from OCD. They will experience what is to be feared as external: the alarm sounded by their OCD is like an air-raid siren. The reality is that the alarm sounded by OCD is more like a claxon sounding an alert for a submarine: what is experienced is internal, anxiety threatening from the darkest depths of the brain.

Looking at it another way, it is as if the sufferer with OCD will have a bizarre thought—is there anyone who has never had a flash of the weird and unwanted?—but discover he or she has a brain full of "sticky paper" that cannot let go of the thought. The average person will shrug off the weird thought; the neurotic will be entertained by it; the impulsive inspired to act first and think later; but with OCD the sufferer has been given a chemical booster shot. In the blare of the chemical alarm, a reflex thought then spins out a scenario of guilt and despair. The quick surge of chemical crisis responders is shocking even if partially recognized as a false alarm; all too easily, the religious person mistranslates this as God

---

*For those who wish to learn more about the brain and OCD, a fascinating book is Frank Tallis's *Obsessive Compulsive Disorder: A Cognitive Neuropsychiatry Perspective* (New York: John Wiley; 1995). Another extremely interesting work is Daniel Siegel's *The Developing Mind* (New York: Guilford Press; 1999).

threatening hellfire and damnation as the fiery neurological messengers whip through. It is as if a primitive something clings to the feeling that an olden god is still displaying his or her wrath. If so, the sufferer has had ample opportunity to know that no ritually offered sacrifice will appease that god or goddess for long.

The way to learn to pick the lock on "brain lock" is first becoming aware more quickly when it is happening. The next step is testing that the misery-making jet stream does stop running through the body given time. Step One: Identify. Identify. Identify. Step Two: Time and verify. Time and verify. Every time the chemicals are resisted, the sufferer is demonstrating having learned how to pick the lock quicker.

This leads to an important consideration for the healing of the sufferer. A number of years ago, there was a conception about psychosis termed "split personality." It was often applied if a person seemed "crazy," but the realization of the physical basis of psychosis made the term appear irrelevant. In the case of OCD and the reality of a "Real Me, Yet Not Me" condition, the term has more validity. We realize that the "split" is not in personality but in levels of awareness. OCD represents an identity challenge on a profound level: the mother loving her baby yet fearing she will harm the child, a father questioning whether he unknowingly committed incest, an honorable person dumping an article in the trash that he or she has compulsively stolen. All the greater and lesser anguishes of OCD represent the challenge of *What is most real to me?* As one of our support group members affirmed, "I have this awful fantasy line running in my head, but I have learned to just go ahead and enjoy my time with my family." The split can work for you, rather than against you.

Martin Luther, as a man of his time, had his own answer: he would throw his inkwell at the devil and shout, "But I am baptized!" The doubting disease is a house divided; healing commences as a determination for the integration of what is neurologically splitting. The caring person supports the sufferer's own pull toward wholeness.

LOOKING CLOSELY AT HOW OCD AFFECTS THE PERSON

Neurological Implications

1. One complication is that *the sufferer will have difficulty in separating thought from behavior.* Thinking the thought is physically experienced as genuinely as if the behavior had been carried out, for the thought is combined with the chemicals arousing it. It is not the thought that is real, it is the chemicals that sustain it; those chemicals are in play and it is this process that feels, and is, overwhelmingly genuine. This is the "real" that undergirds the questioning whether the window is locked, and the dialogue will continue as long as the chemical processes have not dissipated. When they do dissipate, as they always do, then the wretched question of the door being locked, the windows closed, the stove off, simply disappears as well. The potentiality of threat vaporizes: "ordinary" reality will eventually gain ascendancy until the next time. The wheel turns; our task is to find a stick to poke into the spokes before the wheel starts spinning and the person starts obsessing. This cycle is not unusual; a person who has been in Alcoholics Anonymous probably can speak to this helpfully. In many people with OCD, such a cycle can be helpfully identified as well.

2. Healing begins for the young person or adult when he or she grasps the freeing reality that he or she is suffering from a *neurological* disorder, as biological as diabetes: "I'm really not nuts!" Logically, the person knows full well he or she is overreacting; intellectually this is acknowledged by all but 5 percent of sufferers. One key to coping is the realization that the chemicals responding to a crisis evoked from the innermost recesses of the brain lack irresistible might; they not only inadequately represent objective reality, the chemical basis of the "crisis" is perishable. The attack of the mistaken molecules is miserable but temporary. The sufferer needs to become a clock watcher early in the game. Here putting it off another two minutes is success, sheer bull-headedness a triumph.

3. Another aspect of this is that *logic is a weak reed upon which to lean*. The mind has the responsibility to perceive accurately, but another, initially more forceful part of the brain, has *almost* all the power as it thunders and blusters in its rebuttal of logic. In the beginning, the realization of the start of an OCD attack will have only the quality of an academic exercise; the awareness is merely that (in all probability) the dark speck on the doorknob is not an AIDS-infected drop of blood. One is intellectually aware that the ritual is no protection, but the mass in the midbrain insists that it hears the footsteps of pallbearers outside the kitchen, and that somehow arranging the labels on the cans in a certain way will make them go away.

The trancelike state of OCD can deepen, and an outsider can only be aghast at the exaggerated responses: nobody's hands could be *that* foully polluted after repeated soaping, but the sufferer can wonder about it cognitively only after the fixation passes. The key to picking the lock is alertness and action *prior* to the full flow leading to the fixation. Logic here is a weak tool but not without a built-in resource: there is actually a brief moment before the alarm of the midbrain can begin to stimulate the nerves leading into the area of mind. But if the person does not know about it, he or she cannot begin to use that knowledge. This has consequences.

4. When the individual is *prone to unmanageable anxiety,* a dialogue begins: "Run for your life!" "Why? "Where?" "Who?" "Don't ask, run (or fight)!" When this worrisome dialogue starts looping back and forth in a circle between basal ganglia and orbital frontal cortex, the obsession has begun: "Warning! Germs on hands." Sirens blare, red lights blink, glucose pours, the brain seems to speed up, and blood pours into the forehead: "Think quick!" Then comes the attempt to settle down: into the shower, count, tap, arrange the cups with the handles painstakingly just so, see to the exact placing of shoes in the closet. If orderliness doesn't do it, reach for the next bar of soap, and repeat you must, until cleaning descends into red-raw hands, and the passage of time and chemicals permits cessation. The skin cracks, aches; it matters not. Soon the wailing of the germ alarm will sound again.

5. Listening to the basal ganglia gaming the neurological system, we can understand *why persons with OCD tend to have a*

higher than average IQ: they desperately grasp at all the logic they can to compensate for the greater force of the biological. The side effect is that these persons tend to be overanalytical; they will think a thing to death in the chronic course of the doubting disease. An awareness of too many options often produces a potential for a higher level of imaginative functioning, just as perfectionism can lead to high-quality workmanship. The challenge to pastorally care is how to help the person turn a negative into a positive.

What also is lacking and must be cultivated is emotional intelligence. This provides perspective on values: this is worth the worry; that one is not worth the upset. "Don't sweat the small stuff" is not an essay required on the SAT for college entrance, but it is a display of an order of intelligence that is vital to healthy living.

6. *Trapped as OCD sufferers are by a sickening spiral of reconsiderations,* however, indecision spins nightmarishly out of control; even a menu in a village café has twenty opportunities to pursue the ideal choice for today's lunch. It has a drastic effect on mood. Everybody's.

For the hoarder, sorting through a pile of junk mail sets off a courtroom-like debate between two gravel-voiced legalists contending mightily for different clients: whether a sales catalog should be pitched becomes a constitutional issue to be argued up through the courts. A range of interests grows to be beyond the well-being of that person. The need to retain what is potentially important becomes moldy indeed. Run-of-the-mill newspaper articles turn out to be emotional heavyweights too vital to be thrown out, even if not functionally important enough to be actually read. The task of deciding real worth is too, too, too intense; organizing these what-ifs, I might's, and but-I-may-need-it-some-day comes to mean coupling chaos and befuddlement with exhaustion.

At the other extreme of the continuum, scrupulosity, looms a tacky god who is a moral and ethical fussbudget. Is it any wonder why an intelligent person discovers a rage at such "religious" sensations? It is one thing to be a dedicated Methodist or a Muslim, but quite another to be an OCD "Shouldist." The effect of compulsive "honesty," for instance, usually has about the same effect on a marriage as a locker-room practical joker with a can of itching powder.

7. The reality is that there is a degree of angst that forces the gate open between the parts of the neurological circuit we are discussing. OCD makes evaluating the validity of the alarm a horrendous chore. Backing out of the garage can become like having an adolescent gang in the neighborhood who loves to give the fire department a hard time. It is loads of fun for the gang to see them blaring down the freeway to an emergency. For the person with OCD, when the alarm sensors go off there is no automatic evaluation of reality, but rather a frantic chemical "rush" resulting in check and recheck the rechecking, circling the block, or stopping the car and slowly walking back a quarter mile while scanning the ditches for a body. Even getting to a support group meeting can be an act of moral and physical courage to be appreciated.

8. *Blatant magical thinking and superstitions* that an outsider might easily acknowledge are not usually recognized by persons who are blindfolded by OCD. A person may prefer one type of gasoline, but OCD may dictate that in order to prevent some harm, the person may be compelled to go to different gasoline stations. With OCD, life is just one long road full of black cats crossing.

It is not uncommon, for instance, for the person to fear certain numbers, such as 666. If it is seen on a license plate on the way to the support group, the person may be convinced some ill fortune will befall a member of the group. If the word "witches" is seen posted on the bulletin board of the children's section of the library, a spurt of fright may be felt. Logically, a sufferer with this form of OCD realizes that if a "bad" word or number bullies its way into his or her mind, no one will be hurt unless a "good" thought is repeated over and over, but the uneasiness or guiltiness of allowing this thought to happen, biologically speaking, cannot be stopped. Helping the sufferer to name a superstition is a wedge the caregiver can use in the separation of the real from the spurious.

Such magical thinking is highly likely with the too-heavy traffic circling between the inner brain and the outer forebrain along that lowest circuit. These seemingly unfounded sensations of threat may well arise from some primitive memory of war, death, and plague below verbal recall. Such sensations intrude into the here and now, sensations of a "once upon a time" that may have reflected life situations but are now only physically felt echoes. In

OCD these dreads surface and, despite being at odds with immediate perceptions, the brain forces an association between long past and present. In pastoral caring the task is to put into context sensations of dubious validity.

9. In OCD, the swing between consequences and realistic perceptions of what is real becomes an ordeal almost beyond bearing. It is as if you took a microscope and looked at a drop of water from an old cistern from which you had been drinking. OCD embellishes the reality to the degree that none of us would ever want to drink from one again. It is little wonder that those with OCD live like Noah with one ear cocked for the rains to begin. The forebrain doubtless developed its function of foreseeing in order to beat the odds against survival.

OCD EASILY COMBINES WITH OTHER CONDITIONS

An additional set of complicating factors can also be appreciated: a number of *other mental health conditions often commingle with OCD* and may front for it. The top four mental health problems in America are: (1) alcoholism, (2) depression, (3) phobias, and (4) OCD. The order of occurrence in OCD is somewhat different.

1. *Over and Over Again* states that 51 percent of persons with OCD suffer from phobias.* A complication of this is to distinguish these from avoidances.

2. The most generally discussed comorbid condition is depression. Anyone having to cope with OCD is highly likely to feel hopeless (due to the chronic nature of OCD), pessimistic (because he cannot prevent the obsessions and compulsions), lethargic (because OCD is a condition that consumes glucose), and alienated (due to maintaining secrecy). A counselor may not look beneath the depression, and the person may be highly agreeable to

---

*Fugen Neziroglu and Jose A. Yaryura-Tobias, *Over and Over Again: Understanding Obsessive-Compulsive Disorder* (New York: Simon and Schuster; 1995), p. 204, #33.

sharing only a more socially acceptable depression rather than admitting he has terrifying obsessions or "little things" that he "just does" that would make him appear silly.

3. It has been maintained both that alcohol is widely used in a self-medicating way and that a significantly smaller percentage of persons suffering from OCD drink than does the general population. Research can be cited in which the percentage of alcoholics with OCD ranges from 6 to 10 percent, but one study came up with 24 percent. The agreement, however, is that it is high and ought to be a consideration in determining a complete diagnosis.

4. Other health conditions also easily camouflage OCD: a student cannot give full attention when obsessing and may be thought to have attention deficit disorder.

5. The enormous glucose consumption may lead to fibromyalgia. "Fibro" is not infrequently seen in support groups.

6. What appears to be constant worry may be readily confused with generalized anxiety. A spousal complaint of being married to a worrywart may warrant a second opinion.

7. A surprisingly high number of persons come to a support group who suffer from the bipolar condition. For this reason, the consultant in a support group needs to have a good working relationship with a psychiatrist with expertise in OCD. (When on a good bipolar medication, the person also having OCD can do quite well in a support group.)

8. Hypochondriasis is one of the OCD spectrum disorders that may be seen in support groups. In this the person exaggerates physical sensations and obsesses about them as health problems. Even the best physician may want to refer and run, for there seems to be nothing he or she can helpfully treat. The sensation is within the range of normal, but no amount of reassurance can obtain anything but a passing acceptance.

The issue is angst—and that medical and pastoral caregivers are so often caught up with the "real" sick that the sufferer with hypochondriasis is a sight in the doctor's waiting room unobserved and a cry in the night unheeded in the church.

One of the most pressing of national health care needs is a means by which unnecessary health care costs run up by this anxiety are curtailed.

WEEDING OUT UNPASTORAL CARING

At this point, we can begin to see what is questionable in religious practices. The first criterion of a healer is knowledge of what *not* to do. The next chapter explores what to do, but for now it is important to recognize several areas of what is unhelpful.

1. *Afflicting the afflicted with more anxiety* deepens the problem. Religious themes focusing on guilt and punishment have a role in confronting the hard of heart, but they illustrate the "law of unintended effect" with the overly sensitive and those of too-tender conscience. If one of the parents has the doubting disease, a browbeating 11:30 a.m. sermon on the radio about how the fear of the Lord is the beginning of wisdom is not apt to enhance this family's togetherness at 12:30 p.m. at Sunday dinner. Dread whipped up in the forenoon persists into the afternoon as a mother stares at the menu, her mind fearfully spinning about making a wrong decision. Religious teachings adding to the load of those already deeply burdened have been highly questionable ever since gospel writer Matthew set pen to papyrus.

2. *Pushing people to be less realistic, more speculatively oriented in their beliefs is not helpful.* Theology plays a mandated role in religion, although at times it becomes overly speculative and high flown. Inciting the imagination, no matter how religiously phrased, usually reinforces the tendency toward overblown fantasies of those suffering from angst. In the Old Testament, that earthy saint we call Amos exalted the mighty streams of true religion as having to do with justice and righteousness. The New Testament letter of James (1:27), that no-nonsense apostle, stated the standard for healthy religion in worthily concrete terms: caring for the widows and orphans and keeping unstained by wicked behavior. The highly vivid damnations of some preaching need to be consigned to those whose imaginations require more vigorous stimulation than those suffering from anxiety disorders.

3. *Implying unworthiness because of the condition of doubting is unpastoral.* It must be a beautiful feeling to have faith beyond doubt and to be free of ambivalence, wavering, or qualms. Alas, mostly we mortals never attain absolute certainty, however deep

the yearnings. Our goal in pastoral care is to help persons sustain faithful behavior even as they wrestle with overanalyzing, over-responsibility, and oversensitivity. For those in pastoral care, if living with a reasonably high level of assurance, care must be taken that reassuring people that we have doubts, too, does not come across as sounding insincere.

We can say, thanks to what we now know, that the person with OCD is suffering from conflicting sensations so exaggerated they leave the person wrapped in doubt like a fishnet, floundering about trying to determine absolutely what is real. "Is the lock locked?" "Were the pants I just washed contaminated by touching the door of the dryer?" "Am I homosexual?" "Do I have AIDS?" "Am I damned eternally if a damnable thought flashes through my mind?" A solidly behavioral discipleship is highly desirable, no matter of plodding in theological niceties.

If well-intentioned, caring persons, in trying to help, offer guarantees beyond question, they need to realize the questioning nevertheless continues with biological doggedness in the brain beset with OCD. If the caregiver offers theological theory, no matter how intellectually sound and personally satisfying, it may simply reinforce the sufferer's sense of being unable to embrace the caregiver's reality. "Oh, I have my doubts, too," may be meant kindly, but unless the sharing is empathetic it may be heard almost as a taunt by the sufferer.

4. Now the precaution: Never ask for what you do not need to know. Anxiety is universal, but compulsions are often very peculiar—embarrassing often, humiliating sometimes. Obsessions can also be bizarre and occasionally a pit of legal quicksand. Unless you have great confidence in your legal position, never launch an interrogation into anything about which you would not want to be cross-examined by a lawyer.

5. Yesteryear's "pop psychology" is outdated. To be helpful, we must understand that the person with OCD is not simply suffering from a lapse in memory but rather a neurological problem. OCD can be thought of as *a biological experience of the here and now in which ordinary reality is cutting in and out.* OCD sufferers are unwillingly impaled upon a disordering, exaggerated realization. It is just possible that the speck on the door handle is actually infec-

tious—wildly improbable, but not impossible. Unfortunately for someone with OCD, a gate has been left open on a circuit in the brain. All of us have to set reasonable limits on our freewheeling imaginations, but the sufferer from OCD has a vast unease about what is real that is beyond the setting of limits. It is the good news of the caregiver that a person can live healthily with what is beyond certainty.

6. It is important not to rely solely on cognitively learned pastoral authority. Jesus had authority to forgive sins; many clergy regard this as an authority conveyed to them by him. This theological position has to be differentiated from giving reassurance in matters of OCD and scrupulosity. It is impossible to forgive sin where by definition there is no sin! When the source of the problem is neurological, then reassurance, no matter how authoritatively given, will be a temporary "fix" and will result in a continuation of the same process.

OCD, and its subtype of scrupulosity, must be treated by measures appropriate to that disorder; in OCD, "grace never overcomes nature." On the other hand, for persons less vulnerable to anxiety, pastoral reassurance is a great blessing. If the person has scrupulosity, however, and you tell him to "take two aspirins and call me in the morning," he will. Scrupulosity is the equivalent of being a guilt-saddled moral hypochondriac. No matter how religiously phrased, telling people to just "get over it" will not work.

SUMMARY

Knowing now what we know about the brain, we are in a better position to speculate on the actual effects of threats and punishment. That approach is scarcely better or worse than the pastoral pat on the head.

Chapter 6

Helping to Manage the Conflict

A PASTORAL ORIENTATION

1. *An initial task in pastoral caring is identifying and addressing curiously comforting practices.* The result will be the identification of a compulsion. At times it may not fit neatly into a diagnostic category, such as compulsive shopping, but it will be worth considering by a caregiver. We wonder at such compulsions as staring at each and every label on food cans to find the one label without a flaw, but such efforts should be recognized as grasping at straws. Persons with OCD are drowning with anxiety; they cling to a compulsion as if it were a life preserver.

By now everyone can deduce that the ways in which OCD can find expression are apt to be as creative as common, as variable as an individual's history. The basic condition of anxiety arises from heredity and takes shape from the individual's circumstances. This results in unique attempts at relief, whether by picking the skin off fingers or toes or by some addictive offshoot, such as a mental ritual to daydream of heroic deeds and salacious seductions.

2. *Pastoral caring means forever updating one's expertise.* Those who were taught a one-dimensional theology will have to decide whether it is a blessing or a curse to try to rise to the challenge of helping someone stuck with an obsession or a compulsion and in need of a growth model. "To live is to grow," as one of our early support group members was fond of saying.

This is true of all helpers. Some well-meaning counselors of yesteryear tried to teach sufferers to swim by behaviorally throwing them into water over their heads by dictating homework assignments that were too difficult. It is easy to see that effective treatment with OCD today is different; it is one baby step at a time. To be treated today is more like being taught by an experienced swimming instructor, with careful sequencing and encouragement to take the next step as mastery is gained. To give support pastorally is more like being the good parent at the swim meet, offering encouragement and a warm towel as needed.

We are seeking to work cooperatively with what can feel much like being phobic, as in "afraid of the water." To those lacking experience with OCD, it can seem to be merely being frightened of shadows, and the naive urge is to say reassuringly, "Don't worry." The problem is that what is *heard* may be something like, "you scaredy-cat." Persons with a pastoral-care understanding have an advantage here, for the realization is that we are not only working with dreads of a neurological kind, but we understand, thanks to a grasp of scriptural stories, that we wrestle with an angst as long running as our ancestry. Today's balance of logical feelings versus emotional feelings may have ever so slightly shifted, but it is still overwhelmingly weighted toward dark, shadowy feelings, as all the storytellers knew it to be. In pastoral caring, we draw on the old insights, as well as the new.

3. *There are many roles in ministering, for caregivers are part of the priesthood of all believers.* Some persons find a place in evangelism, many in social services, others in preaching, teaching, or administration. They are called to various pastoral roles in the priesthood of all believers; the ordained pastoral role is not that of physician any more than that of pharmacist. Each person in pastoral care must be clear as to the dual nature of the role he or she plays and must respect the unique dimensions of every profession.

We must also be clear as to the pastoral goal: the intention of the person in pastoral care is to help the sufferer achieve a sense of security in the real world that is broad enough so he or she may become greathearted and large minded. If we aim to enable the sufferer to become "a harmonized person," our objective is perhaps unrealistically high, but, on the other hand, if we are slack in our aim we may concede to a view of a human as Ralph Waldo Emerson is reputed to have said, "up a tree and in a squirrel hole."

The role of the pastoral is at times a modest one: to arrange a ceasefire in a civil war where the issues are of long standing. The evangelist may strive for total conversion and the spiritual director for an evolution toward holiness; the pastoral person, more modestly, sometimes is grateful for inner civility so the next small step may be achieved. There are aspects of that ministry where the pastoral especially encourages reaching out for allies (including making a referral to a support group) and educating (for in the pastoral role we teach as well as learn), but to minister within the pastoral offices primarily requires a person whose heart reaches out to those who neglect each other, brother ignoring brother, a mother compelled into self-absorption, a father unmindful. The pastoral task requires a person whose mind is large enough to encompass both the tradition of the Faith and contemporary scientific thought, with a heart sufficiently accepting of the individual that a model is offered to those suffering from a torment of what is most intolerable to each of them.

Let us now turn toward developing areas of competency in coping with this inner conflict that is so far from civil. If one were to take the long view about living in this "house of clay," it would be that of a co-worker in God's reportedly most ambitious and creative project, Out of the Dust of the Earth.

DOING THE WORK OF PASTORAL CARE

1. *The first area of competency for caregiving is that of helping the sufferer manage doubt.* The most dubious technique for this is offering the good advice that would be quite suitable for the worried-well. Often the person with OCD is also depressed, and the ambivalence inherent in depression reinforces the doubt inherent in OCD. The person needs to know that the saints, too, passed through the "dark night of the soul" when the sufferer feels not only alienated from others, but also from God. If some doubting Thomas becomes familiar with the lives of the saints, he or she can rest secure that OCD does not mean a would-be believer is AWOL from the ranks of the Church Historic. For years John Bunyan, author of *Pilgrim's Progress,* was tormented as he wavered in his

ability to believe the promises of Scripture that he was saved. Having doubt as a believer is no different from being scared as a soldier. Being scared can keep you alive, and doubt can be God's tool for creative advance. What has to be learned is that obsessing is most often worth nothing: mere overanalyzing. We are called to act in faithfulness rather than waiting around to perfect and protect ourselves.

2. In OCD literature, the usual term has been "intrusive" (we have used "reflex thought" as more descriptive) to describe unbidden and unwanted thoughts: if you prefer the historic term, why should we not interpret this as "temptation"? Is there anything newer than what we are learning about the brain/mind, or anything older than the struggle between flesh and spirit in our historic struggle to discipline the flesh? It is helpful to be supplied with new tools by scientific thought and psychological insight.

In working with "temptation," we can now add the tool of identifying avoidance. We can recognize a new aspect of biological pressure in giving in to the seductiveness of the "flesh"; in running from it we can run into something that may be fully as ruinous. The temptation to overindulge one's body is no less real in caving in to an obsession or compulsion than in nursing on the brown nipple of a fifth of Old Grand-Dad. The life of the spirit has always required self-discipline in regard to temptations. In the pastoral care of those with OCD, this is helpfully becoming more refined.

3. In working in this field, it will also be apparent that the sensations of religion as often have a free association to a Grand Inquisitor as to a Heavenly Father. Is there a more ancient and honorable task of spirituality than *upgrading the willy-nilly sensations of "religious" false condemnations?* Is there any greater pathological silliness than a father using the electrical prod of scrupulosity on one of his children for some piffle of thought or deed?

4. For those in pastoral care, there are well-trod avenues to be explored. Law and grace are to be compared, fastidiousness versus graciousness, legalism against kindness. But there are now fresh avenues to explore as well: reflex thoughts floating out of the "left field" of the innermost brain can be contrasted with behavior that is freely and willingly determined. The choice of being free in Christ can become as real as the differences in glucose consump-

tion photographed in pre- and post-PET scans during OCD brain studies. It is, however, a freedom lived out only by a disciplined, knowledgeable volunteer.

5. In reaching toward freedom, occasionally someone with OCD will be fearful that he or she is somehow entangled with what was identified in the Old Testament as witchcraft. This is not unnatural, considering the various superstitions to which this disorder is heir, such as, "If I think a bad thought, something bad will happen." *Superstitions and magical thinking are two of the curses inflicted by OCD.* Of course, no witchcraft or black magic arises from a reflex thought: simply compare a voodoo doctor sticking pins in a doll to what is felt by sufferers from OCD and their horror of doing harm. Can you imagine anyone with scrupulosity concocting a love potion? What is helpful in working with OCD is to identify the various ways in which this disorder strongly resembles primitive superstitions. When pointing out that some childhood games have aspects of rituals, the issue is not citing what is childlike.

> Step on a crack and break your mother's back,
> Step in a hole and break your mother's sugar bowl.

Rather, it is similar to placing an example of magical thinking under glass in an anthropological museum.

6. *Perfectionism* is the bane and blessing of religion, and part and parcel of OCD as well. To live perfectly according to God's holy law is an aspiration that has beckoned many a saint—and occasioned a not inconsiderable number of pitfalls. It has also kept many anxious believers from sleeping while trying to get that prayer said *exactly* so. One of the pastoral skills has to be developing an acceptance of those ever-risky feelings surrounding *good enough*. A cognitive-behavioral therapist will recognize a pastoral colleague when he or she hears pointed out to a sufferer, "The Perfect is the enemy of the Good." OCD may be a chemical imbalance, but this proverb can help a life become less of ride on a rollercoaster.

7. Another all-too-common obsession with which we all must sometimes cope is the *fear of death*. If a person does not have some fear of death, it is more likely to be "it can't happen to me!"

than a blissful faith. The problem of so many with OCD is that having the thought is like being hung out to dry, while the rest of us are preoccupied with it only situationally. The person in pastoral care can help with the reality that *a fear accepted is a fear that becomes increasingly manageable,* even if while we live it never goes beyond some next corner.

We had a group member whose OCD was exceptionally severe and which began with a fear of death after one parent died. Then the other parent was diagnosed with a fatal illness and had to be taken into his or her home for a last year of life. There could be no avoidance. What must be, must be: acceptance. Then the fear of death began dissipating. It was an inescapable—very brutal—exposure and response blocking. The OCD remained but was greatly modified; what became enhanced was a new sense of empowerment as a person—which was shared with others.

8. A key pastoral skill is to recognize things for what they are. OCD is a strange disorder, full of contrasts and extremes. It colors everything in the gray of doubt for some and makes all things totally black or white for others. In hoarding, all things seem of equal worth; in scrupulosity, trifles merit thunderclaps of wrath from olden gods. To measure, to see in perspective, to explore the *in relationship to,* all these are pastoral skills to be shared.

9. Fortunately, there is an accumulated wisdom from our religious heritage, particularly regarding obsessing about guilt. There is a pastoral tradition concerning "mortal" sin, which is sin that threatens the health of the soul. Catholic tradition has strict criteria for a sin to be mortal. One: it has to be serious. (For many OCD obsessions, this is too easily met: "I fear I may kill my baby," or "I fear committing incest.") Two: it must be considered at length. This, too, is easy with an obsession, although it is one thing to have a thought from which you cannot escape and another thing to get pleasure from it, as in an addiction. Third: it has to have *the full consent of the will.* Have you ever heard someone with OCD willingly agree to those thoughts?

Persons with OCD can appreciate a story about the great English thinker Samuel Johnson and his scrupulosity. His best friends once found him with his arms wrapped about his pastor's knees, begging the pastor to keep him from going crazy. Enlightenment philosopher or computer programmer, eighteenth century or twenty-first, Anglican or Pentecostal—or German, Columbian, Chinese, Australian, and Austrian, then as now: does not our heart go out to encompass those so burdened? How much more so must it be for a Heavenly Father, creator of heaven and earth, who has framed our bodies and whispered guidance to our minds. Is not the responsibility ultimately his for perfecting us? And yet, has not he chosen us to be his co-workers?

RECLAIMING OUR PASTORAL HERITAGE

1. The first piece of pastoral wisdom to be reclaimed is, devoid of its Latin phrasing, *Do what you are doing.* We are to unify a splitting of awareness, restore an integrity of purpose, give weight to the mind by concentrating on the awareness of the ordinary always available to it. The medieval saint Brother Lawrence is a marvelous role model for this. His duties in the monastery kitchen were avenues of prayer. A trip to the village market was an opportunity to be open to the awareness of God. If a more psychotherapeutic term is wanted, try the phrase "conscious sensations" to describe the technique of the enlargement of awareness through encompassing more of immediate reality. The ancient wisdom is to give full attention to the here and now. The modern technique is to slow down when checking the lock: move slowly, touch it, bringing all five senses into play. Apparently the private devotional life of C. S. Lewis, a saintly sufferer, made much of this. The point of such conscious sensations is that reality is precious. The "ordinary" is essential to spirituality in managing the dark whirlpool of angst sucking at the person's grasp on a larger reality. Take a walk: smell the newly mowed grass on a lawn, watch a cloud, feel the solid earth under your feet, embrace the rhymes of your heart. That magnificent modern Quaker mystic Rufus Jones was a master of this, and his books deserve the attention of those dealing with this disorder. Was it not St. Augustine who wrote, "Without God, Nothing is strong?"

You may have noticed the mythic quality of OCD. It is as if the Brothers Grimm had spun a fairy tale called "The Woman Who

Imagined She Could Be Perfect." OCD can be like a trance in which the person washes on and on toward some fanciful purification beyond concrete experience. It is like daydreaming in which by counting in sevens or elevens, the potential ills around us are forestalled. One of the techniques of dealing with obsessions is to elaborate in great detail what is feared. In the case of obsessing about death, this might come right down to the smell of the flowers on the coffin. There is nothing like a heaping tablespoon of reality to settle an upset imagination: repeat as often as needed. For God is the ground of all Reality.

There is a mysticism that is a trap, a way of negativity, a self-induced trance far too similar in some ways to OCD itself. The religious discipline that is most hopeful, a way of positivity, builds on what is commonplace; it is an openness to an awareness of the Real through the mundane, such as the multiple sensations of turning the key in a lock. *Do what you are doing.* Bathe your senses in Reality. Interestingly, if the compulsion is to shower on and on and on, if the person has an important appointment it is rare that he or she will lose track of reality. It is the Truth, a greater Reality, that sets the person free.

2. The next saying also comes from Ignatius of Loyola, who knew himself what it was to deal with obsessions and compulsions: *Do the opposite.* It took an earthly while for exposure and response blocking to be developed by behaviorists; meanwhile, spiritual directors were encouraging sufferers to confront their problems directly. It is still good advice from a modern spiritual director of whatever credentials. Direct action against the problem is hard-headed common sense. If temptation nags someone to keep circling the block, the sufferer knows the right thing to do, and a modern spiritual director knows what to support. Neither does it take a mastery of yoga or Sigmund Freud to be a genuinely helpful group member.

3. The next piece of pastoral wisdom requires some adaptation for many persons: the sufferer should stay with one confessor, rather than jump from one to another. What inhibits helpful actions is that persons with OCD readily chase not only second, but third and fourth opinions; this is especially true with hypochondriasis. In this context, Catholic pastoral manuals advise having

only one confessor. C. S. Lewis, himself an Anglican, found this recommendation freeing; blessedly, he discovered the pastoral advice given to him was always simple and straight to the point.

This simplicity and straightforwardness is necessary to counter an OCD fact of life: the human brain can be expected to produce some peculiar electrical spikes every once in a while. That first OCD "hiccup," however, continues into an excruciating process and then into the maze of doubting. From there, add two or more well-intentioned advisors and mix well with contradictions to create always-lurking doubt. As the Germans quip, and this is supremely true of OCD perfectionism, "cut three times and still too short."

4. In connection to the difficulty that persons with the doubting disease have with third-guessing themselves, it is traditional pastoral advice to find a sensible person to consult concerning the flopping around in OCD of decision making. For those troubled by scrupulosity, the interesting thing is the word traditionally used to describe that adviser: "prudent." Many terms could be used, such as "mature," "far-sighted," "wise," "having good common sense," but the older pastoral manuals state *prudent* and prudent it is for those of us who are heirs to the rich inheritance of pastoral caring. The modern term has an association with bankers who make loans or do investment counseling—actually a pretty good choice of words when dealing with OCD as a "paralysis of analysis." "Prudent" has a fraternal twin called "good enough," because we all have to place our bets somewhere or risk losing it all.

5. Then there is that ancient treasure cherished by those in recovery from OCD when, as Christians, they have fallen into line in obedience to their marching orders: "The just shall live by faith alone." It is this, rather than some ritual such as reliance upon the straightening and refolding of a washcloth, that makes for a more abundant life. In discussing the mystery of the sacraments, Martin Luther stated a conviction for all those for whom there are no absolute certainties: "Melanchthon, we must trust God and sin bravely!" This is true about the unknowable quality of the sacraments and true for a woman with a compulsion to turn all the handles of the cups in the same way to prevent a calamity befalling her family. If the lady in question happens to believe in the devil, she

should turn those cups every which way, spit in his evil eye, and dare him to do something about it. Pastoral lore has a grand tradition of advocating reality testing.

6. Crucial to this reality testing is to face a difficult pastoral challenge: the adequacy of our personal understanding of what it is we term "Higher Power," as the Twelve Steps of Alcoholics Anonymous puts it. All too often, the "god" that is experienced during an OCD episode is one more suitable to a Hollywood director's fantasy of a pagan idol on a jungle island, complete with scanty wraparounds and throbbing tom-toms. In the splitting of awareness, intellectually the sufferer is squeezed into tunnel vision; existentially what is experienced is primeval. The god felt by the person with OCD is a god that is too small. The spiritual struggle of caregiver and care receiver is to become mutually open to a Reality adequate to healing: a wholeness, a oneness, a stand taken within the broad traditions of one's faith. *The pastoral need is to help in the discovery of a Creative Power adequate to heal both mind and brain.*

CALLING UPON MODERN INSIGHTS

Much that is new remains to be learned; for those in pastoral care, one of the most precious promises of Jesus before he was taken from the disciples was to assure his followers that he would send the Holy Spirit to guide them to more and greater truths.

1. We need to remember that the reflex thought is simply an isolated neurological event, no matter how sexually kinky, religiously repugnant, or eye-poppingly distorted; it is purely and simply morally neutral. A reflex thought is only an interpretation of an unusual electrical spike, raising in that atomic instant no ethical questions. Obsessing is similar to having hiccups. Period. Now let us get on to better coping skills and management techniques for preventing the obsessions from creating a choke hold on the mind. That is where the pastoral action is. If the sediment at the bottom of the middle brain causes too much misery, call for an evaluation for medication: finding a different route to success is no insult to a heavenly Father.

2. As our tradition has taught us to value reality and cherish the ordinary, we can build on this and pass it along. For the compulsion to check a lock, the person might imagine that the door handle is a clock and look at five o'clock instead of directly at the middle of the handle; it is a part of reality that we have blind spots in our retinas. Move in slow motion, and practice awareness. Breathe. Suck in real life in all the physical senses.

3. Part of our new learning is that "food is medicine and medicine is food." Scurvy was conquered when lime juice was added to sailors' daily fare; now we may take a vitamin C tablet for convenience. Not infrequently, some sufferer has reservations about taking medication, usually based on someone else's theoretical opinion. It is helpful for the caregiver to affirm the reality that both food and medications are composed of chemical elements and there is no more spiritual justification for not seeking an optimal chemical balance in the body than there is for not eating the best possible nutritional diet. Goiters were eliminated by iodized salt, and tooth decay is challenged by fluoride. Would that tomorrow's medications would get here today!

Thinking back, in the Middle Ages there were saints who strove for holiness by refusing food or by existing on bread and water for years. Today we might wonder about anorexia; eating disorders are far too commonly linked with OCD. Certainly the spiritual director of today would not encourage anyone to go on a 500-calorie daily diet, no matter which holy person of yore opted for it. Rather, we are free to encourage any sufferer who experiences his mind habitually speeding up to forgo caffeine, and to discuss a serotonin reuptake inhibitor with his physician if his anxiety is such that homework assignments cannot be carried out.

Because enormous glucose consumption in the brain is one of the hallmarks of OCD, we would also be wise to encourage anyone suffering from the disorder to forgo the quickly absorbed sugars and to level out the ingestion of calories throughout the day. Many persons with OCD become "chocoholics," as the sugar supplements deplcted glucose and the chocolate does supply some serotonin; the problem begins with other side effects. Good nutrition is good health, good religion. Every religion has tried to move in that direction, although religious leaders until recently could not have known how food and religion combine for the most benefit. They tried, and God bless their memory for it! We now know some; with open minds and good research, we will learn more.

4. Another new learning is that we particularly benefit the sufferer when we keep firmly in mind that OCD is a neurological issue, not initially a moral or ethical problem. The empowerment of the person begins when we center the issue on the modification of undesirable thoughts and behaviors. When the obsession is acknowledged as grounded in biology, then the person can look forward to feeling much more normal as the obsession and consequent compulsion are modified. If, on the other hand, the obsession and compulsion are somehow attributed to dark, demonic forces, as if this somehow was "spiritual," then the sufferer is indeed condemned to suffer. The anxiety underlying the physical manifestation of OCD is never going to completely go away any more than the person is going to start living apart from his or her physical body. A public track record exists: exorcisms have failed, while cognitive-behavioral therapy, with its exposure and response blocking, has a reasonable success rate, on occasion with a boost from medication. Not perfect, but good enough for now.

5. With the knowledge that OCD is grounded in anxiety, it is clear *why so often prayer has missed the target.* If the prayer is directed at the obsession, the aim is too high; if the prayer is directed at the compulsion, the aim is even worse since the compulsion functions to dampen an obsession. An answer to prayer in either case would evade the vital, if troublesome, human quality of anxiety. Now we know: *the bull's-eye for prayer is anxiousness.*

The best answer to prayer is to do something about the trigger that lets loose the obsession: being too tired, too hungry, too sleepy. The person rising from prayer with greater self-discipline has had his or her prayer already answered. A partial answer is, "Be still and wait," for a fuller answer is, "and this, too, will pass away." On average the chemicals then run through in less than an hour. The "average," however, is individualized. Some pass in ten minutes and some in two days, but the chemicals do pass. Prayer gives the power to wait.

If the reflux sensation rises to the fright of being homosexual (or having AIDS or committing incest or...), at some point comes a time of acceptance of the underlying angst. After all, when all is said and done, the Creator has written and read the proofs on the entire manuscript of sexuality. If the compulsion is to touch a picture of Jesus before leaving the house lest hell bellow and famine follow, is not the challenge of prayer to identify the superstition and take it easy, in God's name?

6. We also now know: *Don't fight the white bear.* If we liken an obsession to a white bear, the old tried-and-true is to try concentrating for five minutes on *not* thinking about one and seeing how that succeeds. The same happens with all obsessions—the more they are fought, the more tenacious they are. Obsessions are like the Chinese handcuffs made out of bamboo strips: the more you struggle, the tighter they grip.

You may remember the story of one of the labors forced upon the Greek hero Hercules. He had to wrestle and overcome a monster, but every time he threw it on Mother Earth it became twice as strong. He won by holding it over his head until it starved to death. The sufferer from OCD cannot win by wrestling it. The winning tactic is to passively accept it and it will gradually modify.

Too often the result for an aware adult sufferer is an explosive debate similar to deciding whether the sonar has picked up an enemy submarine or a whale; in OCD this can go on and on and on. We see the same thing in Alcoholics Anonymous. People go from obsessing about drinking to obsessing about not drinking. Result: a dry drunk and a slip waiting to happen. The pastoral care solution: do not get bent out of shape about a chemical-induced belch from the basal ganglia. What we do not do is regret that we have a warning system; God is predictably not about to perform that kind of psychosurgery. One task of pastoral care is to assist in the adjustment of the warning system so that it becomes more functional.

7. Part of the gift the person in pastoral care brings is the good news of just-don't-get-so-hot-and-bothered; pastoral caregivers help *put things in perspective,* such as the reflex thought. Although some such thoughts would gross anyone out, they are nevertheless part of a temporary process in God's adventurous program for us individually. We are human, and God is in on that. He is also still in on bigger things such as justice and mercy and caring about widows and orphans and war refugees. He doubtless wills

that we quit sweating the small stuff (such as whether the prayer is grammatically precise). An answer to prayer always involves action on the larger issues such as, "Thy kingdom come. Thy will be done." "Beginning with me" is often added for the benefit of reducing angst.

People with OCD volunteer, too, although realistically some can and some cannot. Perhaps while a mother is praying about her fear of doing harm, one answer might be serving in a children's hospital. The only danger is to her OCD. On one level, OCD is a pattern of self-absorption: the counterattack is to enlarge the individual's interests.

8. *We encourage realistic behavior.* A driver with OCD may have a fear of doing harm, and consequently drives staring into the rearview mirror to check that no one has been run over. As a teenager once remarked, "My OCD is awful strong, but it sure isn't very smart!" A therapeutic injunction is much like the good advice of a parent in Appalachia when the child goes off to school: "You act smart now!"

Often, wannabe believers ask the pastorally caring person to read a portion of the Bible to them. Because we are dealing with anxiety, the wisdom literature of the Old Testament, such as Proverbs, is often good. Mark, Luke, and John are more often helpful, while passages from the Book of Revelations or Daniel are more apt to illustrate how aspects of religion sometimes "go to bed" with an anxiety disorder.

9. The use of Scripture is particularly helpful when it is directed toward the characteristics of the disorder, such as perfectionism and superstition. "Salvation by fearfulness" is the undercover motto for both the lay and religious perfectionist. "Say this prayer ten times and you will be healed" fits better into superstition than worship. Another example is being overly analytical: you must be as a little child to enter the Kingdom of Heaven. For the overly responsible: you are to love your neighbor as yourself. Self-neglect, just like self-mutilation, deserves pity rather than the name of piety.

10. In the way of new *learning about vulnerability,* we can use the matter of blasphemy, for we can learn even from this kind of reflex thought. On the matter of responsibility, first, it is angst that

is the ground for the unusual electrical spike; the person did not will it. Second, the sufferer is, however, vulnerable to stress and that may have made him or her open to a bizarre spike by getting too tired, too hungry, too sleepy. The person does not want the spike and has no responsibility for its occurring, although he or she does have a responsibility for making the body less vulnerable. Each person is held accountable—literally—for controlling his or her lifestyle in a way that tends to keep the spikes from happening as often. Third, OCD strikes in the areas where our deepest values lie. What OCD blasphemy actually signifies is that religious values are truly precious to this particular person. Think about it: the fear of doing harm at a deeper level reflects the principle, "Love your neighbor as yourself." It marks a significant spiritual advance from fear of harm to the self to a fear of doing harm. Finally, avoidance also echoes these values; the blasphemies often occur in church, and consequently felt as a need for avoiding some trigger. This also targets the treatment. Such blasphemy may fool the blasphemer, but it does not fool God any more than hypocrisy does.

To use C. S. Lewis as an example, we do not have more than clues as to his obsession. We do know he always sat behind a pillar in church and left before the service was over, but he was consistently in church for worship and his writings have benefited us all. The author of *The Screwtape Letters* is a classical example of turning an overly imaginative quality of OCD from a negative into a positive. He was able to master and moderate his wildest fantasies into disciplined narratives (Narnia books), such as his stories of Aslan, the lion king.

11. There is another aspect to *OCD striking at a person's values;* healing climaxes when a person begins to explore what he or she is really about. This is the strength of the climactic step in *Brain Lock*: clarifying what is most meaningful to the person. Values shift as the sufferer explores his or her life meanings with a pastorally concerned caregiver. Obsessions arising from primitive survival fears (not too dissimilar to the checking and rechecking of any wild animal) begin to shift as they are transcended by what is more profound to the person.

12. One final caution for those in pastoral care: a sufferer once flung a charge at a person who expressed what was felt as a too-personal interest in OCD: "You're just interested because you want to hear about all the silly things we do!" Many compulsions sound silly, but the secretive obsessions rarely are. The caregiver always remembers the underlying angst. The compulsion is like a plume of smoke that is visible over an active volcano. The compulsions are never trite, simply offering something that, to an outsider, seems unlikely to be comforting; but then, we do not have the sufferer's biological makeup.

SUMMARY

So as we take our place in an endless line of splendid caregivers, let us remind ourselves of the proverb common among Swiss mountaineers: "We climb on the backs of our fathers." We have a magnificent heritage, if selective, to share with those who suffer.

Chapter 7

Putting It All Together

SCRUPULOSITY: WHEN SHARP-EDGED MORALISMS PUT A SPIN ON RELIGION

We of the Church Universal have not managed this disorder well. Prior to the ecumenical council known as Vatican II, scrupulosity was an acknowledged burden borne primarily by Roman Catholics and centered on the confessional. A practicing Catholic could not receive the sacraments without making a comprehensive confession. Every priest recognized parishioners who were scrupulous because of trying to keep fastidious rules beyond what was required for receiving the Body and Blood. The poor person with scrupulosity might come to the confessional booth writhing with angst at the thought of having not flossed her teeth sufficiently the night before. The priest hearing this sort of religious nit-picking also writhed. One priest described hearing confessions in a convent as akin to being pelted by wet balls of tissue paper. Under the leadership of the great John Paul I, less significant regulations were modified and pastoral care probably improved, as many priests now wanted to talk over a parishioner's pain in the office rather than through a vent screened with a cloth.

The problem, of course, is that simply because persons suffering from scrupulosity may no longer "bug" the priest, it does not mean they no longer suffer from outlandish concerns gone ballistic. It certainly has not done anything for the atheist with OCD and torments of nonspecific hellfire; he or she has been left with all the fire and no explanatory clause as to the hellishness of it. Protestants should make our good confession here: many of us have been too busy with our revival meetings to puzzle over those who felt the necessity to be converted every time an opportunity presented itself. As to a good church member suffering from contamination fears who might have to throw away a new purse and pair of shoes if caught out in the rain on the way home from a church committee meeting? Never heard of it.

Yet we have all known someone who goes after the tiniest flaws as if they were body lice (most often his or her own but not always, for scruples can reach such an intensity that they become projected onto others). Ordinarily, persons look askance at those who, when confronted with a white wall, see only the flyspecks. It is important, though, to realize how painful it is to be forced to concentrate on flyspecks. Having said this, let it also be said that the scrupulous, however exasperating their examination of the fine print may be, are nevertheless worthy of respectful consideration. Consider the scrupulous lawyer reading a contract for you before you sign.

The reality is that we have a continuum here. At one end we have conscious values, which are one monument to our humanness. Then come our principles, from which we exhibit our ability to think logically and abstractly and which potentially lead to the heroic, but also can become those small sharp rocks in the shoes of the masochist. At this point, we begin to wonder about the role of martyrdom in history. It is at this extreme that we find scrupulosity, the moral rack upon which the perfectionist is stretched. It is also time to reflect on how masochism and sadism often are flip sides of the same coin.

Beyond this point is aggressive scrupulosity, when the scruples become communal in nature and are readily projected, aggressively so. Given their repetitive historical occurrence, one would suspect that aggressive scrupulosity is latent in any society. Our immediate pastoral concern, however, is with the scrupulosity of the individual.

A SCENARIO FOR SCRUPULOSITY

No one knows the actual process of scrupulosity, of course, but for purposes of discussion let us consider a theoretical scenario. The person's name might be Bobby or Bobbie, Billy or Betty.

With OCD the symptoms are charitably distributed in matters of sex as well as fame, fortune, or color of the epidermis.

To begin, let us assume that almost all of us have scruples to some degree if we have a sense of conscience at all, that scrupulosity exists on a continuum, and that it is capable of intensifying, for bad or good, under stress. Scrupulosity is a potentiality in the human condition and awaits only the situation.

Scrupulosity will not come into its fullness, however, except under two conditions: a genetic predisposition to more than ordinary anxiety and under circumstances of sufficient stress to surface that level of anxiety. The basal ganglia will supply the vulnerability to anxiety; it cannot, however, create scrupulosity. It can only give it a commonality to OCD. For scrupulosity to arise, an external authority must impress upon the forebrain those values and principles that will give shape to the underlying vulnerability when the occasion arises.

The "raw material" of the individual destined for scrupulosity probably begins with being highly sensitive to others, having an active intellect, and being unusually responsive to moral and ethical considerations. This, however, is an overlay: beneath is a genetic grounding in anxiety sufficient to exaggerate these virtues into tormenting vices, certainly to oneself, and potentially to others.

Thus we can anticipate that for the individual there will be a before and after condition: before there is only the vulnerability caused by worrisome anxiety, and after the stress has opened the door to consciously experience a deeper level, angst. What begins is the scruple; what transcends is the scrupulosity, both of which have to be taught. The high drama of scrupulosity is what attracts the attention of mental health personnel. It goes without saying that the scripting and casting of the drama is of intense concern to those in pastoral care who share the role of custodians of tradition and values.

In one possible scenario, this Billy or Billie who will develop scrupulosity is reared by "good" parents, and they have a very "good" child. The parents are likely to be God fearing and religion is valued in their home, but what they communicate will interact with a genetically transmitted vulnerability to anxiety. In a worst-case scenario, that underlying vulnerability will be intensified by what is taught by the parents or community.

Instead of what the psychiatrists term "an overvalued idea," such as having committed the unforgivable sin, we have instead an "overvalued value." The result is a heightened degree of conformity to parental religion, honoring of parents, or duty to country, perhaps even "obedience, obedience, obedience." That value, given the magnification of stress, would then be greatly exaggerated. The person would suffer from a scruple whenever that value was somehow agitated, and suffer more if that value was threatened. Anxiety would distort the sense of what is of worth "out of kilter" for Mary or Maria, Esther or Sook Ja.

We will explore this primary route more exactly, but first we need to acknowledge that at any point in the process we are considering, circumstances might produce the level of concern that would produce the transformation of scruples into scrupulosity.

This process quite possibly takes on its exaggerated shape due to a meticulous and judgmental parent, parental authority, or tightly bonded society, often with a religious "flavor" stirred into the psychological mix. The scruples will be rigorously taught. This gives a black-and-white characteristic to thinking, an unguarded potentiality for love or hate, a stiffened stance of "us and them." It can also lead to a serious case of uniqueness, as a group member with an AA background liked to phrase it.

Out of such a parenting situation, a few children openly rebel, a few acquiesce until later in life, and a few become part of the worried well. When this form of OCD is the outcome for a vulnerable child, this "mix" is accepted and internalized, for the sake of argument, as an expression of love and care, even if the parenting is heavy-handed. Eager to be accepted, the child becomes overly compliant.

When the judgmentalism of the parents, as a side effect of their strongly held values, combines with the oversensitivity of the child, the result is a very "good" child, but perhaps a Bobbie or Bobby prone to what is dismissed as nervousness.

Since the excessive standards of parenting are presented to the child as being for the child's benefit, too often the person later intermingles wanting to please with self-neglect, potentially self-hurtful thinking and behavior, and certainly unquestioning guilt. The child has become too good for his (or her) own good.

The crucial time for this to occur developmentally in the child's life is from age thirty-six months through five years, which coincides with the time when a child having a strep infection may begin exhibiting symptoms of OCD and also when the child wants to have the same book read over and over in exactly the same way. This is a time when the child shifts from identification with "basic family" to a later identification with a male figure, the father; it is also the time of the internalization of conscience. It is a time when the parent unquestionably seems godlike, and also when the image of God seems masculine and consequently tends to be more rigid. A consequence of this is that the ideals of the parents will be accepted as if they were the Word of God, and the rules, as perceived by the child, will be like Scripture. If the setting is an authoritarian society, the mores of an idealistic religious group may have highly specific expressions (such as how to dress), created from assumptions not to be questioned by the child, who later may become highly vulnerable to feelings of threat from the larger world.

The individual's underlying anxiety increasingly produces exaggerations as the child's world enlarges, so that what might have been normative community ethical and moral teachings become moralistic searching for flyspecks. Now sin is seen where there is no sin. A later crisis in growth in the teens or early twenties may become a time of dedicating oneself to even greater conformity.

In attempting to satisfy these internalized demands as they become exaggerated, there are now too many details with which to cope as the scope of life broadens. The attempt to be perfect leads to a sense of greater and greater uncertainty, with no lessening of a need to please. An emotional undercurrent of doubts has begun but is suppressed, even denied.

Again, let it be said that there is no time line for the transformation of scruples into scrupulosity. It may occur due to a biological stressor or emotional stresses. The effect is that an unstable dominance of the forebrain area is undermined and the balance of power shifts to even greater openness to the forces of the basal ganglia. What was a respect for the traditions of the elders can become a crusade against some outside threat.

Reality begins to become fuzzy in its outlines as the person becomes more ambivalent about being able to satisfy any questioning. One strategy for coping is an increasing emphasis on closed group participation—back to the basic family developmentally, in its adult form "back to basics." Another outcome would be to define the articles of the faith, insist on conformity, and aggressively defend these basics that were internalized so early. Just as doubt is denied, so doubters are suppressed or scorned.

There is now an attempt by the person, and this can have a panicky quality, to both live with internalized demands and cope with the demands of external reality. In the process, reality is meticulously analyzed, broken into smaller and smaller units for a sense of safety, and then finally compartmentalized. The focus of attention increasingly narrows as the scrupulous person attempts to grasp perfection, or to defend an imagined group perfection, all the while feeling queasy because the reach exceeds the grasp.

The person's uneasy centering usually shifts into a repudiation of what has been taught or a greater acceptance. In this acceptance, the tendency is to become unreasonably humble as an expression of low self-esteem or to be self-righteous beyond any logic. In either event, certainty becomes an ever-increasing need, a searching for flyspecks on the white walls of one's inner home, fearing they will be found—and of course provoking them. The need for reassurance, of course, also steadily increases. An externalization begins.

The end result is the loss of the big picture. The defective conscience of the scrupulous has come into being. We see this in the Gospel according to Matthew where the worry became the scruple of eating from a ritually unclean dish or eating with unwashed hands rather than the impurity that comes from within the person. A traditional longing for a purer self or purer society can become a panicky search for a better germicidal soap for the self or society.

REFLECTING PASTORALLY ON SCRUPLES

Thus we see that scrupulosity grows out of idealism but runs beyond it as a pathological response to angst. It is the urge to escape judgment by pleasing, being "good" literally beyond what is sensible. Going to church may gestate scruples, but it does not necessarily give birth to scrupulosity; given certain vulnerabilities, an anxious atheist can be tormented by the sharp edges of flinty scruples as easily as the most pious of true believers. The person simply has become "too good for his own good," merciless with self-condemnation and expectations.

1. Integral to scruples is a conscience, or *what has been overlearned as conscience,* that is located not in the lofty reaches of the mind but in some sort of mental halfway house in the brain subject to constant interrogations by the doubting disease. Necessary to this, of course, is a lurking Grand Inquisitor, whom some would unquestioningly call god, until someone begins carefully to slip in the appropriate questions about what is authentically sacred.

2. From a purely Christian perspective, we need to *raise the issue of heavy-handed scruples when the requirements of faith exceed those of Jesus in his teaching and example.* To refer to the example of Jesus is always a good reality check. Since Matthew is cast in a scrupulous cultural setting, the pastoral caregiver gains an edge in focusing scriptural quotations on Mark, Luke, and John. The Apostle Paul in his letters was consistent in reflecting on scrupulous religious requirements: freely quote Paul, the apostle facing a larger social reality.

3. The person with the torments of the trivial is in *need of a measure of what is "good enough" and "normal,"* as difficult as these are to define. There is always a need for a prudent person, solid in common sense. It is not farfetched for the person in pastoral care to use as a mantra, "I love reality," and enlist allies for that. The trick often is to use insightfulness.

4. There is also the fundamental biological issue of *the chemical imbalance.* This is not an alien concept to those who realize we are made from dust and to dust we shall return. The counterpart to this chemical imbalance is a social imbalance, that gray area *giving birth to both self-abasement and self-righteousness.* The challenge to pastoral care in the issue of imbalance is to help the person hold on to the paradox of a realistic estimate of one's goodness in both directions, for both humility and rectitude are justified and necessary.

5. It is wise to differentiate *strategic interventions* in a dysfunctional situation from *tactical interventions*. As a clinician, interventions are most often tactical: for example, having the patient make a tape recording and then play back the obsessing until he or she is completely bored. As an example of a strategic intervention, a newcomer to a support group was given the suggestion that she read *Brain Lock*. She had the book but was unable to endure reading it. Her husband had come with her, and so a group member turned to him and suggested that he and his wife read a few pages together out loud every night when they went to bed. The tactical is narrowly prescriptive; the strategic, a characteristic pastoral approach, is more suggestive than prescriptive, often including others in order to broaden the person's resources.

6. Finally, in my judgment, *the construction crew for the highway to healing is composed of empathic individuals*. Pity has small place in pastoral caring. Soft-headed sympathy merits a shake of the head. We all have our aches and pains and all have, or will have, some knots on the ego. It is out of empathy that a feeling for the neighbor comes that facilitates healing. How often in a support group I have heard it ever so graciously said: "Yeah. You're family, all right."

SUMMARY

We can be deservedly modest about what we can achieve, but that is not unsubstantial, as we are about to see as we explore a helpful component of pastoral care, the support group. Religious commitment in the small group is demonstrated by empathy; it is in relationships that we find highways to healing. In relationships, opportunity arises to infiltrate the space of an anxiety-sealed sufferer. Peace, however biologically shaky, can have its spiritual awakening in such fellow feeling.

Chapter 8

For Those Wanting
to Go the Second Mile

PASTORAL CARE IN A GROUP SETTING

Pastoral caring usually is carried on in private, but the context of that relationship, even if one-to-one, is a larger community. In pastoral care, we recognize that our area is not private religion but community service out of religious commitment.

Because so much of the content of OCD has religious implications and associations, inevitably the subject of religion is an active one. For a support group, the trap is that in fumbling for words to express intense, nonverbal sensations, some persons are tempted to recite doctrinal formulas as if these had powers in and of themselves. This alienates others, of course, rather than helping them share their personal strengths and weaknesses, which builds community. This makes for walking a line: on one hand the subject of religion must be addressed, but on the other, the way in which it is addressed is crucial, as OCD is characterized by a narrowing, excluding focus, even a rigid, aggressive one. A different approach must be taken: the therapeutic way is to walk that line by staying in a widening, accepting style of thinking and relating to persons: broad minded, large hearted, gracious. This is the pastoral *context* for facilitating the healing of the split between mind and brain, the person's thoughts and behaviors. This is *context,* not a group therapy methodology for OCD treatment. In a relational setting the emphasis, first of all, is on pastoral style, rather than pastoral technique.

A mission statement for such a ministry through a support group would emphasize, first, a religious orientation toward relatedness, rather than "God talk." The symptoms of OCD often lend themselves to religious jargon and the wordiness of piety, but it is in the sharing of pain and concern for one another that we find a relatedness raising us to the heights of genuine religious expression and experience. Who knows better than someone with OCD that a pound of compassion for the self and the neighbor is worth a kiloton of psychobabble or pious wordiness?

MODELS FROM THERAPY

There are several therapeutic group models from which to choose, such as a treatment/support model, often associated with an OCD treatment center. In this model, the almost exclusive focus is on sequential treatment targets associated with an individual's OCD; social needs literally come at the tail end of the meeting. A crude comparison might be made with Weight Watchers; the person chooses a goal, openly writes it down, and is supported by and accountable to the group in attaining it. An excellent video on this model is available for purchase from the Resource Center of the OC Foundation (see Appendix A). Professional leadership is highly desirable for this model and could be a useful extension of the ministry of pastoral care in a mental health setting.

For those wanting to set up a group with perhaps a more personal growth focus, a model utilizing a format familiar to many is that of Alcoholics Anonymous. This has one advantage in that many alcoholics suffer from OCD; perhaps their drinking unwittingly served the purpose of self-medication. Some addictive drinkers may not be able to maintain recovery until the underlying cause, OCD, is addressed. It is certainly probable that the experiences and learning from AA will benefit any OCD support model that is chosen. Again, an excellent updated book on OC Anonymous is available from the OC Foundation. The case histories are outstanding and will remind persons familiar with AA of *The Big Book.*

Both of these models are demonstrated at the OC Foundation's annual convention. A support group demonstration was annually given until the leader became the executive director of the OC Foundation. Whatever model is used, it is essential to keep in mind that the only approach that has been successfully developed so far combines both the cognitive and the behavioral, and considers when medication is needed.

A third resource, one that may be underutilized by many suffering from OCD, is the National Alliance for the Mentally Ill (NAMI). There are over 1,200 chapters in the United States. NAMI chapters ordinarily serve those who are profoundly disturbed, such as those with bipolar disorder or schizophrenia. At the same time, many persons with OCD are severely ill, and not infrequently, OCD combines with other categories of mental distress. Usually the meetings of our local chapter are broken up into small groups at an appropriate time, which often includes a separate group for the family and spouses of the mentally ill. If too few persons with OCD live in a given area to have a support group solely for that disorder, some linkage is in order.

Having said this, let us move to a different model, one that is flexible and can be drawn upon either for private practice or a not-for-profit ministry.

OUR SUPPORT GROUP EXPERIENCE

As another possibility, a description of the Fort Wayne OCD Support Group offers talking points for persons considering how best to serve sufferers in their area.

Fort Wayne, in northeast Indiana, is a city of 200,000, a metropolitan area of half a million, served by two local daily newspapers and four television stations. If 2.5 percent of the population has OCD and needs treatment, there would be about 12,500 in this area. Our group draws individuals from this whole area and actually beyond, as referrals come in from the OC Foundation. These frequently come from their Web site, and usually there are several per year. We have found it difficult to draw from minority groups, but a variety of faith groups, and nonfaith groups, have participated. Inquiries predictably come in after any mass media presentation about OCD and increasingly from searching the Web. Of the local pastors who might make referrals, Catholic priests may be in the best position to do so immediately.

The group began in 1993 and has had perhaps 250 to 300 participants at weekly meetings and special events. It meets in a church across the street from a large high school, so identification of location is usually not a problem. The room in which we meet is nondenominational, and the religious affiliation of individuals appears not to be a hindrance. We have a basket on the table for donations and usually give a couple hundred dollars annually to the local church in appreciation for the use of the room; any mailing costs are minimal. My home telephone is listed in the "Here's Help" column of the local newspapers.

The group was begun out of my caseload as director of the Samaritan Pastoral Counseling Center. I worked with a great number of pastors over the years and became aware that OCD is a significant dynamic in the lives of many religious persons. As I moved toward retirement, I wanted to maintain a small private practice and do some volunteer work. When my wife and I went to the first national convention of the OC Foundation, we decided it was a cutting edge of the mental health movement, and the intellectual stimulus of being part of that intrigued me. I did not mind getting older, but had no intention of being old. I became aware, too, that—being very frank—people with OCD tend to be nice people, if anything too responsible, and usually do not have to be hospitalized just when a counselor wants to go on vacation! Perhaps a semiretired mental health professional might be found to act as consultant to a support group; a certified pastoral counselor with interests in OCD might well be especially valuable since religious issues are so widespread.

A half dozen persons began the group, one of whom was a referral from my family physician, with whom I had discussed the project. Fortunately, we caught the public relations tide when OCD was a popular topic in the national media; I called the local television talk show people, and they gave us air time to describe OCD and to discuss the need for a support group. The daily newspaper published an interview, and the public radio station was especially generous.

In terms of my participation in the various public forums, I had not anticipated it would result in building up a caseload in semi-retirement, and it has not. For me, it is ministry. I enjoyed seeing some people in the media I had known as the director of a mental health center, and that enjoyment made the effort more than worthwhile.

The television interviews were taped, and the first was aired at 5:30 a.m. on a farm program! The person referred from the doctor went with me; he was a sales executive for a major corporation and was nearing retirement, a man of scrupulous integrity at work and a leader in his church. When I arrived fifteen minutes early, he had been there for half an hour. He explained that that was what he had to do for every meeting. After the show, he simply went back to the office and told the staff about his OCD, and he has said he was never late for a committee meeting afterward.

We had two others who allowed themselves to be used for publicity purposes in getting started: courageous acts. I say "used" because they probably suffered for their willingness to serve others. The executive was in a position to withstand any cheap shots or reservations about potential adverse public fallout from the appearance of an employee; the others were less so. In discussing publicity for the group, or some group member sharing his or her OCD with fellow employees or even other professionals, our group experience suggests being cautious. Relationships on a line in a factory can be as wearing as the work itself.

An interview on public radio was noteworthy because it got around the publicity problem to an acceptable degree. Five members of our group told their stories; because it was radio, all could be reasonably anonymous. One more did not come because of fears; something like this could be expected and did not diminish the success of the experience, nor did it diminish the respect all of us have for that individual. As she gained in strength, she went on to a caring ministry in her local church.

We had one large media event after about two years. We wisely chose to make it a cooperative event. A well-known expert in OCD, a seminary professor and member of the American Association of Pastoral Counselors, Joseph Ciarrocchi, came for a day-long seminar at the Catholic cathedral. It was sponsored by the makers of Luvox, a corporation that has been very generous to OCD educational events. A mailing list from the Association of Churches made it possible to contact clergy in a hundred-mile sweep; each was asked to bring an interested mental health professional. Two hundred persons came, including persons from a broader area who had seen the notice in the OC Foundation newsletter. We did not particularly build our group from the event, but as the consultant I answered a variety of telephone calls for a whole year afterward.

The support group meets on Mondays from 7:00 to 8:30. Both starting and ending time are important as structuring the meeting time is therapeutic. Persons with OCD need encouragement to resist becoming involved in an anxiety-reducing ritual before leaving home, such as checking or changing clothes. The size of the meeting varies from six to twenty-six; ordinarily about eight to twelve are there. About half are regulars. Others might include a person coming for a "booster shot" or perhaps a newcomer (often with a family member or friend). It is worth noting, if size is a concern, that a small group is occasionally beneficial; a member who is habitually silent will often use those meetings to do his or her work. It is also worth noting that as far as possible, we meet fifty-two Mondays a year. Holidays are stressful for those with OCD and often significant help is rendered at those times. Groups quickly develop their own leadership. The only contractual requirement is that some person be present for all meetings who is a member of the local church; this meets their need for security.

We have an annual reunion in May. This birthday of the group is an occasion for a mailing, and persons return to share their experiences. It is a rewarding time, both for the maintenance of gains and to offer realistic hope to newcomers of being able to live more normal lives. It includes a potluck, accompanied by good-natured teasing about contamination fears. This teasing has itself become a ritual concerning the threat level of a person (who has a terror of doing harm) who was afraid she was going to poison us all with her chocolate chip cookies. It begins a month early, and of course she would not dare miss that meeting.

We usually have one newcomer every other week. Some stay for a while; some do not. All, however, appear to benefit in that they learn they are not alone; often they are welcomed as family, with a chuckle, "Yeah, sorry to tell you, but you're not crazy!" It is not unusual for a person to sit for a long while in pregnant silence; then someone senses she or he has frightful fantasies of evil. When the emotional dam bursts, sometimes after years of being held in solitary confinement, someone will quietly say, "It is okay; you're with family now."

Persons come and stay according to their needs: our ten-year veteran comes once a month and brings a passage from OCD literature he has been reading. A four-year veteran comes one meeting in six and has a new poem. Three or four will be there regularly for a couple of years. A mother may come twice or thrice to discuss where to find help for her adult son; a wife may come to the group, instead of going to a lawyer, in order to learn how to better cope with an anxiety-throttled husband. Another person may come on recommendation from a therapist to evaluate the intensity of his OCD (and perhaps discover to his glad surprise that, in comparison, things are a lot more manageable than he had imagined).

There are some group issues that need recognition. One is advice giving. Individuals come who are treated by various therapists. It is an ethical issue not to interfere with that relationship by thought, word, or deed. In order not to mute some participant's freedom of speech and yet observe the ethical proprieties, I try to informally shape group rules on this issue.

Medication, too, is an issue, for nearly everyone wants to talk about it. It is a forbidden topic as to any implication as to what might be hinted as a prescription; it can be a helpful topic when a sufferer is phobic about taking any. Doctors write out what they want; patients take what they are willing to take. A group can be helpful here. A person who is terrified to swallow that first pill can bring the bottle and take the pill at the beginning of the meeting. We are there for such persons.

Most often, both new and old members bring their immediate stress to lay on the table. Although OCD is the focus, stresses are so interrelated that we hear the person out. It simply is not allowable, however, to continue to express an obsession. Talking about a divorce for an hour may be accepted once. Starting and being unable to stop in a second meeting gives rise to a question. The third week it gets confronted. Throw a pity party and no one will come.

It is a rarity, but sometimes a newcomer will be so pressured that he or she overexposes by blurting out so much that it would be difficult to return for a second meeting. If the consultant senses this is happening, then a tactful suggestion is made that some silent members may have something on their minds; that sort of comment can be very helpful.

Meeting social needs is clearly secondary on the group agenda. This does not mean, however, that they are insignificant. Having OCD is an isolating experience. Being a part of a community of hope, direction, and support is very important; exercising one's almost atrophied social skills is therapeutic. Silence about what is most pressuring is not golden, but radioactive.

None of the group goes to any one physician or psychiatrist. None of them goes to any particular counselor, and any and all are welcome. The purposes of our group are self-directed therapy for OCD (and sometimes related issues for which there seems to be no other community resource) and, secondarily, learning about OCD in the context of group relationships. We have even permitted students from advanced psychology or nursing courses to participate as their fieldwork assignments; usually by the end of the session the interest is admitted to be personal. Some sufferers come and almost immediately go into individual therapy, while others come after individual treatment for maintenance of gains. Since many physicians offer medication but not cognitive-behavioral therapy, the support group experience offers a necessary supplement to the medical relationship.

As a footnote, in my private practice I have worked for some time with a psychiatrist and naturally have made referrals to him. Although over the years group members probably have seen every psychiatrist in town and felt good about it, still it is natural there has been some gravitation to the consultant with whom I am most familiar. Since anyone working with significant numbers of one type of client develops an expertise, it would seem helpful in any situation to cultivate one psychiatrist so that some specialization develops. There is no prejudgment to this, simply a matter of determining who has a particular interest. It is possible that a psychiatrist might be found with OCD or who has a family member suffering from it.

It is inevitable that on occasion some participant will begin to voice disappointment with some physician or counselor. We have not found this to be a problem. In our experience, the group handles this in a mature way. Usually we simply hear out the complaint, and then the group discussion turns another way and continues.

It is an open meeting, and some families will come as a support to a member undergoing intensive therapy. Socialization occurs for the isolated, triage for the severely disturbed, and consultation by both group and consultant is offered when family and friends seek help. No one is referred away from the group but rather is incorporated, to whatever extent this is realistic.

There is no therapeutic model for the group. Care is taken by me that the cognitive-behavioral approach is understood and encouraged. The book most often mentioned is *Brain Lock: Free Yourself from Obsessive-Compulsive Behavior, a Four-Step Self-Treatment Method to Change Your Brain Chemistry,* by Jeffrey Schwartz (1996). The first step is often quoted: "It's not me, it's my OCD." Years back, it was I who frequently cited the second step: OCD as a chemical event. Now it most often comes from a member of the group.

When a newcomer arrives, we introduce ourselves by first name only, other than myself. It is explicitly stated that everything said in group is confidential. I tell the newcomer that he or she is free to speak or to remain silent and go on to ask if he or she has brought any questions. Usually, I will look around the group and add, "You have a whole group of experts here." Often the newcomer asks the group members what form of OCD they have. Members speak up with astonishing casualness—after all, even with the multiple forms OCD takes, they tend not to be unique to an individual. It is not long as we go around the circle that the newcomer unconsciously begins nodding. I then may find the timing right to ask the person if he or she does not have another question about that particular concern. Persons most often fall in with the group atmosphere and share freely. The follow-up exploratory questions by some group members are often astonishingly intuitive.

The professional consultant, in this model, de-emphasizes being an expert, but rather draws out empathy and, consequently, expertise out of the group. I find that my restraint is often more productive than my comments. Some group member will offer a better insight than I was preparing to make. Educational lectures about OCD need to be restrained, as they slow group process; encouragement and explanation of exposure and response needs frequent repetition. If eye contact from participants keeps being directed toward the consultant, then reordering of group dynamics needs to take place; if a group does not have a good laugh or two every week, something needs to be reconsidered. In our context, the consultant serves as a leader in group work rather than as a therapist.

A precautionary note needs to be sounded about therapy with OCD. The function of a compulsion is to bind feelings. OCD is listed as an anxiety disorder, but the nature of OCD is such that a dual or even a triple diagnosis would be warranted. It is unwise for a sufferer to act hastily or more especially to attempt too great a leap forward. It is the "baby steps" in treatment that are not only effective but safe. Don't rush, and don't pressure people. Keep a steady course with sharing, empathy, and personal example.

Some persons who come can pose problems. Sexual aggressiveness may occur. Occasionally women in the group may even voice concerns to the consultant. It was on a different issue, but on one occasion later we even heard rumors that the neighbors had made formal charges about a participant; the person, however, convinced the judge that he should be given special consideration because he was going to start coming to a support group. (That happens to AA groups, too.)

A different problem is an in-your-face scrupulosity that can lead to some highly aggressive "Christian" declarations. When such pushiness is joined with reluctance to address one's own OCD, the group is confronted with a difficult decision. Ordinarily, a participant who becomes a group issue usually finds that an experienced group member calls him or her aside for a talk after a meeting. Sometimes it comes to pass that a consultant does what a consultant has to do: suggest leaving the group if the behavior is not stopped. Shouting "Guilty!" in a guilt-packed room has to have a firm response.

One special problem is more related to an OCD group than to most other groups. Persons with OCD have a high degree of needing to be liked. They are often both tender-minded and hypersensitive. For this reason, the dropout rate can be high.

Meetings often close with each participant being urged to identify and accomplish one step forward in the coming week. It is always one step because of the splitting of focus characteristic of OCD. An objective always present is the increasing unity of the personality. Baby steps are encouraged: brain circuitry is being re-routed and patience is encouraged, with small gains celebrated with applause. Always the recommendation is that in choosing what it is someone wants to attack, the consensus is to attack OCD at the weakest link in the individual's chain. Be disciplined, not heroic. To control OCD, choose the time and place where the confrontation takes place and issue the challenge there.

SOME LESSONS WE HAVE LEARNED

As a part of the pros and cons of any model, here are several points to be made from our group experience. These are not "cases," but recollections culled by a group member.

Here was a person for whom the *Diagnostic and Statistical Manual* always leaves a loophole at the end of a chapter: "unspecified." He had always been the odd one. If the class was given a problem in mathematics, he always had the right answer. He just could not figure out how the teacher could come up with her answer, and the teacher was always frustrated because his way never jibed with her way. The diagnosis of an attention-deficit disorder may even have supplied a rationale for getting him through high school. Once as an adult he had worked with an excellent psychologist who ordered brain scans. They suggested his wiring zigged when it was supposed to zag. At some unknown time, however, his brain had adapted so that a new area responded to his need to read. Life had nevertheless been difficult. I am unsure how he came to the support group; with OCD he could talk the talk, but never seemed compelled to walk the OCD walk. Then after about three years the realization came that most of his family had it. He does have some OCD characteristics, but principally he had internalized the family's ways!

He is remarried now and has received recognition from his local congregation. A few meetings ago, we were discussing the five loops in the brain and effect of the excitatory and inhibitory functions of the OCD loop. Suddenly he began to share how he had made his leaps forward: he had taught himself to shift over to "spiritual thinking." He had learned to shift into another loop in his brain.

Point one: The brain is flexible.

The woman was not ready for retirement, competent in the way many with OCD are as they make use of their perfectionism, but also depressed and experiencing herself as very angry, as so many with OCD do. In the course of being a regular in the group, her depression moderated and so did her level of medication; she never had much to say about exposure and response prevention. She just listened. We were surprised, however, when her absence was lengthy one summer. We were more surprised at her termination when she returned and announced a near-cure.

Her husband loved his motorcycle—apparently as much as she feared it. He had always wanted to take a long motorcycle vacation with her "before we get too old." She decided that as much as she loved him, she would just go. She hopped on, wrapped her arms around him, and away they went into the Wild West: talk about your exposure and response blocking! And most of that depressive and fearsome OCD met its sunset somewhere out on the lone prairie.

Point two: Intelligent, informed, courageous self-directed therapy can be successful.

She had retired. Now she sat quietly for a year in the corner of the meeting room, smiling. Her only movement was her pencil as she took notes. Finally, on a holiday night when the church was closed and four of us met at a small restaurant, she began telling her story.

She had been hospitalized soon after marriage and ever afterward her husband and she routinely refilled her antipsychotic medications compliantly. Now she was suffering from the physical aftereffects of sustained heavy dosages. She had always accepted her diagnosis with OCD. For years her family discounted her as "sick." At a meeting soon after we four had met, she suddenly but quietly stated to the group she doubted she had OCD. She left the meeting and went home to her husband and began for the first time expressing herself as worthy to be heard: she was not going to be treated as a mental patient any longer. She next started in on the rest of the family—and her family life is now reported to be highly satisfactory to all.

Every reunion she drops by the group to say thank you. She continues to take some medication, apparently for a lower level of depression, but she is not psychotic. And she always straightens up and states, "In spite of that medication I held down a job and always did my work."

Point three: We may not know all the whys and wherefores, but persons will find help in support groups in unexpected ways.

He came to our annual birthday party to say thank you. He is a kindly, older, very gentle man, a deeply religious person. His wife had suffered from undiagnosed OCD for many, many years. He had bought hand soap in enormous amounts, coping with the illness as best he could. Now she was in a nursing home, her OCD still severe. She came once to the group; she wore plastic gloves, touching nothing, very frail, clinging to his arm for support. He came regularly, lonely, needing to talk to people who understood.

Then she was gone. When our alumni gathered to share how the year had gone, his words were of thanks. With his coming, he said, he was making a closure. His church, I think, was of great comfort to him, but I suspect that it was in our little community that he was able to commune in a time of deepest need.

Point four: The needs of those who suffer from OCD are very broad and a support group can be a community of faith and hope.

She was eighteen and a top high school student when it struck. Now she could no longer read successfully, having to go over and over a paragraph because of her fear that she would not remember it perfectly. Scruples came; she hated God for the torment he sent her. She feared to do harm. Once, when caught in the rain, she threw away her new shoes and purse she had just purchased; they had been contaminated beyond being able to be cleaned.

The clouds began to break some years later when she discovered that she was saved by grace, not by being perfect. When she had to take a long, boring business trip, her counselor encouraged her to take the most fluffy, empty-headed piece of fiction she could find and read it through: exposure and response blocking, and it worked.

One of her children was given an assignment in a third world country; she longed to go, and both counselor and support group encouraged her. The country in which she stayed was, well, "third worldish." She loved the people she came to know and hung her keepsakes on the walls: of course they could not be cleaned, but up they went and up they stayed.

The fear of doing harm remained. It centered on her pet, which she feared would run out the door as she left for work. The fear was so strong that she had an illusion its tail would be caught in the door. Then her beloved pet had cancer on its face. Her contamination fears surfaced. The pain was intense and it had to be put to sleep. The veterinarian came and her pet died in her arms. She was devastated, as everyone knows who has loved such a friend.

Two weeks later a friend called. One of her friends had moved away and could not take her kitten with her. You who have had to put a pet to sleep know the feelings that came over her, but by now you already know what such a woman would do.

Some time later she asked to borrow one of our support group's tapes, *The Touching Tree*.* She was leading the continuing education session that month for a lay ministry group in her church and she wanted to do it on OCD. I would have been glad to give her a text for her talk. It would be from I John 4:18: "There is no fear in love, but perfect love casts out fear."

Point five: The loving heart can move a person beyond "cure" into being healed and whole.

This success story is of the most common, ordinary, garden-variety kind, and therefore of genuine significance. It is about the first participant in the support group, a corporate executive who was a lay leader in congregational worship in his church.

As you can readily imagine, the company hung on to him as long as they could, but golf won. Now that he could play as often as he wanted, there was one problem: he had to stop the play and count, count, and recount his golf strokes to be certain he had not cheated. It was one of those classic moves of OCD that simply make your jaw drop: in his forty-year battle with the disorder he had checked, he had counted, and he had scruples by the gross. Now that he was retired, the OCD combined all three and zapped him in the worst possible way—while he played golf, OCD played gotcha. But he is classic, too. Knowing how to battle and win with OCD, he stayed in there with driver and five iron. He reframed the issue and undercut the anxiety. "It's only a game." He accepted his anxiety and the need for minor soothing and refused—and continues to refuse—to get upset. Once you know how to mute the OCD, it will still recur—inevitably when stress mounts, as it did in this instance with retirement—but as he says to newcomers, "It is never quite as severe. Bite the bullet. Exposure and response does it."

---

*This is a video of a young boy with OCD. It is tender, moving story and one well suited to interpreting the disorder to groups. It can be ordered from the OC Foundation. See Appendix A.

Then he opens some book on OCD he has been reading that week and shares a particularly good paragraph with us. Courage is contagious: when a genetic research program was advertised in the OCD newsletter, the whole family signed up.

Point six: "Love bears all things, believes all things, hopes all things, endures all things" (I Corinthians 13:7).

Permission to tell this story came so late that it had to be left until last.

She had tried every model of psychotherapy available locally as well as some nationally advertised seminars. Nothing worked. She continued going from doctor to doctor, always on the edge of frantic as she consulted her personal library-size collection of medical books. One heavy-duty twinge of muscle or nerve, think-about, think-about, read, read, read, and then on to test, test, test, test in the search for a definite answer to a feelings-induced health crisis. Always there were negative test results and a turned-off doctor. A wider to wilder medical theory only led to a further off solution to this, that, and other pain. She decided to drop in on our OCD support group: "wouldn't hurt." It was clear that she, along with others along the way, was dealing with one of the spectrum disorders of OCD.

As providence would have it, Carla Cantor's *Phantom Illness: Shattering the Myth of Hypochondria* came out soon after and I loaned my copy to her. She duplicated the entire first chapter and sent it to all her close friends with a note saying, "This is me!" Then came a knowing physician ("I only take three persons with hypochondriasis at a time.") and one of the serotonin reuptake inhibitor medications.

At times, she reported later, she had to clench her teeth and sit in the emergency waiting room of a hospital until the urge passed. But the urge would finally relent, as all the OCD urges do, as the chemicals that create them do pass out of the body. Class-act lady: she would then move on to whatever leadership project she had going at work or church.

The reason that her permission to use this story came so late is that it had to be forwarded to her overseas where she is teaching. "Not bad for a person with OCD," her note read.

Rather than making a point about this story, perhaps we ought to regard it as a lesson assignment.

Appendix A

Resources

The Primary Organization

Obsessive-Compulsive Foundation
Phone: (203) 401-2070
e-mail: info@ocfoundation.org

For a Full Listing of Resources

Fred Penzel, *Obsessive-Compulsive Disorders: A Complete Guide to Getting Well and Staying Well.* New York: Oxford University Press, 2000. Chapter 13, "Finding Resources and Getting Help."

A Short List of Recommended Readings

Ciarrocchi, Joseph, *The Doubting Disease.* New York: Paulist Press, 1995.

Collie, Robert, *The Obsessive-Compulsive Disorder: Pastoral Care for the Road to Change.* Binghamton, NY: The Haworth Press, 2000.

Hyman, Bruce and Cherry Pedrick, *The OCD Workbook: Your Guide to Breaking Free from Obsessive-Compulsive Disorder.* Oakland, CA: New Harbinger Publications, 1999.

Osborn, Ian, *Tormenting Thoughts and Secret Rituals.* New York: Pantheon Books, 1998.

Roy C., *Obsessive-Compulsive Anonymous: Recovering from Obsessive-Compulsive Disorder.* Hyde Park, NY: Obsessive-Compulsive Anonymous, Inc., 1990.

Schwartz, Jeffrey, *Brain Lock: Free Yourself from Obsessive-Compulsive Behavior, a Four-Step Self-Treatment Method to Change Your Brain Chemistry.* New York: Regan Books, 1996.

Schwartz, Jeffrey and Sharon Begley, *The Mind and the Brain.* New York: Regan Books, 2002.

For an Academic Study of Group Therapy for OCD

Whittal, Maureen L. and Peter D. McLeon, Group Cognitive Behavioral Therapy for Obsessive-Compulsive Disorder. In Randy O. Frost and Gail Steketee, editors, *Cognitive Approaches to Obsessions and Compulsions: Theory, Assessment, and Treatment.* New York: Pergamon, 2002.

Appendix B

Slices of Life

BRYAN'S STORY

To use sex as an illustration of an obsession, we begin by recognizing that sexuality is a given. In any species it is indivisible from the instinct to survive. If sex were not something of an obsession, we would have neither writers nor readers. To a behaviorist, there are no moral implications to the subject; sex is neither good nor bad, simply a means of species perpetuation, as varied as the species themselves. As Christians, we affirm all creation is good; species survival as such may be morally and ethically neutral, but we affirm the goodness and beauty of God's ongoing creative process.

Now comes the rub: "morally and ethically neutral." For humans, self-consciousness and broadening awareness of others entail the varieties of anxiety and its derivative, the capacity for feeling guilt. It is one thing for the mammal to couple, another for the human to procreate, just as it is one thing for the squirrel to store nuts and another for the mother to alienate her children with hoarding.

Let us now imagine a person, Bryan, with a vulnerability to angst, cause unknown. Now (perhaps because of childhood circumstances?), sexual obsessions have become a "black hole" drawing in energy and consuming it; now we have a person with a reflex thought occurring whenever stimuli occur suggesting sexuality, perhaps while watching a TV commercial with a woman selling home loans by wearing a revealing outfit. The thoughts are distasteful, unsolicited, unentertaining. They can be triggered just as easily in Bryan when a business letter is being dictated or at the copying machine.

The obsessive cycling begins with, as routinely happens to the male of the species, an occurrence of some sexual image. The issue is whether Bryan responds to a knee-jerk feeling of guilt with the conviction that he is damned to hell for a sudden electrical surge. If sufficient anxiety is already in store, the gloom-and-doom cycling begins as if the soul was under threat—a spiritual "outage" is occurring. Since Bryan is a deeply religious person, these painful thoughts are often apt to occur in church.

Formerly, if Catholic, Bryan might have felt compelled to run to his pastor and confess, sometimes frequently. Today he may discover a compulsive ritual of "undoing": he may say half aloud, "But I love my wife." It acts similarly to throwing salt over your shoulder to counter a hex—the rite may temporarily appease the anxiety, but the apprehension (like heartburn) quickly rebuilds in Bryan. By merely having a sensation natural to the male (and female, too), his soul is now at stake; time will stand still until the chemical charges have run their course, while with increasing impatience office staff and his children may wonder why he strangely avoids some things.

Bryan may attempt to avoid the buildup of tension by fleeing any situation likely to suggest a sexual stimulus. His wife may regard him as a saint because she knows he would "never look at another woman."

Bryan knows, however, he is damned to hell no matter what, a hellish living since it is a farfetched longing to get away from manipulative advertisements using sex appeal. He yearns to be free from his torment, to be beyond reproach, not as an ideal but as a freedom, yet he cannot break away, for he cannot evade biology. Now enters self-loathing—he must be weak, crazy, depraved, immoral, corrupt—and depression follows as night the day.

For a while Bryan almost stopped going to church, for what was happening during worship was not the wandering eye of the wayward husband, but thoughts that sickened him. Finally he and his pastor talked. Luckily for Bryan, his pastor recognized that an initiating sensation is morally and ethically neutral. Their joke became, "It's the intention, stupid!" God's evaluations rest on willful behavior, not on an electrochemical malfunction. A brain wave's wild spike does not eternal damnation make; more relevant are good intentions not carried out. That's when Bryan became active in his congregation's lay ministry.

To summarize, if Bryan values those qualities we hold to be religious, then the reflex thought that automatically jumps forth from anguishing sensations will appear to have religious significance. Because the signals have the appearance of a soul-threatening situation, a quality of enormous seriousness is conveyed by them. Genuine religious values do have such a message—to those with calluses on their consciences. The reflex thought is ethically and morally neutral, however, having no religious value whatsoever; the authentic religious response is not in that jolt from the innards of Bryan's brain, but in mature, rational reflection as to what is real and the basis of what he wills. Therein lies the problem of OCD but also the potentiality for a healing process.

BILL'S STORY

To further explore these stages, let us imagine the situation of a high school student, Bill, with football jacket and acceptance letter to a local college, all of which are mixed well with extraordinary anxiety and focused on contamination fears. After some classes, he goes to a school rest room; a sensation occurs there as he sees some water splashed on the floor. The sensation of warning is followed by a reflex thought of "germs" jerking his mind and gripping his stomach. His thought fixates on floating, splashing filth. Of course there is a kernel of truth here (as in every rest room), but the OCD intrusion races beyond reality, literally slamming the door on the ability to get back to class.

Time stands still as he is glued to the sink, meticulously disinfecting and decontaminating as if he were going into surgery, not social science. Unless the ritual is conducted to a mythical absolute, unutterable harm may result either to him or others. It is as if someone had spilled an envelope with anthrax spores and he will be tracking them into class. The class bell rings. He will be late; with his mind paralyzed by now, he cannot stop the sensations as he decontaminates his decontaminated hands. He can perhaps only turn off the water in the sink as another student comes into the rest room, providing a snapback into everyday reality. But now he is staring at the door handle. The last person may not have washed his hands before opening it; it seems to be actually wiggling with germs. He fakes that nothing is wrong, waiting until the other student is ready to leave, and then slides through the door on the other person's push.

Four hours later, avoidance becomes impossible. He must go to the rest room again. He dreads it, and out of experience the teacher is reluctant to let him have a pass to go to the rest room. It happens on too many school days. Hopefully the hunch of the teacher is confirmed by the school counselor, and the discussion expands to the parents and a cognitive-behavioral psychotherapist experienced with OCD.

To broaden the context of Bill's dilemma, and the family's and the school's, hopefully the school counselor and classroom teachers will also confer about Bill's grades. It is obvious to his teachers that he is of above-average intelligence, but his grades are no confirmation. Coupled with high anxiety is his vulnerability to imagine, overanalyze, and to perfect a test to OCD's overblown specifications: Bill has the doubting disease.

Perhaps talking with his school counselor, he will remember stories of how in elementary school he wore out innumerable erasers, in middle school he would never wear the same jeans twice, and now if a multiple choice test is before him he is lucky to get through the first five questions. He can come up with why each of the four answers on each question could possibly be right and possibly be wrong.

In August, the anticipation of school will balloon the national averages for hospitalization of students with OCD; fortunately, the end of the first six weeks represents the beginning of the cooling-off period, but the end of school is scarcely better than the beginning.* Will Bill make it through that first year when he goes to college?

SALLY'S STORY

The same dynamic could equally be used to describe a person with other compulsions. When the fall of the year is coming on and the leaves are coming down all over the yard, you may have seen Sally: after work, and after dark, with a flashlight, picking them up. There she is at the desk, two hours after work, busily perfecting her notes; she is the most dedicated of employees, until it gets to be an annoyance to all concerned. Soon she will be going home to mow the lawn, first one way and then a crosscut to ensure no grass blade escapes. The manicuring is beautiful, if you do not have to do it (or live with it).

Sally did not come in for counseling because of these difficulties, but rather for difficulties with her marriage. For years she had been undecided about getting a divorce. What confirmed the diagnosis of the doubting disease was that she always had her check written out when she came. She felt she had to because of her need to be per-

---

*Tamar E. Chansky's book, *Freeing Your Child from Obsessive-Compulsive Disorder: A Powerful, Practical Program for Parents of Children and Adolescents*, is excellent. The OC Foundation has fine booklets for teachers and parents, as well.

fect. It would have taken her fifteen minutes standing before the secretary to get that check *just right*. Just like it did for every bill she wrote.

In all three stories, the gender could be switched without doing harm to the story: OCD is an equal-opportunity misery. There is another factor to be considered, as well. All three might have learned that the obsessions could be dampened down with alcohol or marijuana. It starts as self-medicating; its ending needs no explanation. When that happens, there is a dual diagnosis, followed by two-layered treatment.

Appendix C

The Spectrum Disorders

Several conditions associated with OCD are called the spectrum disorders. Although they are somewhat less common, a person in pastoral care may become aware of any of these, particularly in a group setting.

TRICHOTILLOMANIA

The first of these is compulsive hair pulling, called trichotillomania. It most often affects girls, beginning in their early teens; the first observation is that a girl has no eyelashes or eyebrows. In other instances, bare patches begin to show on the scalp. The woman suffering from it may adopt a very creative hairstyle to cover a bald patch but is often forced to wear a wig. To learn more about this condition, consult the Trichotillomania Learning Center on the World Wide Web.

KLEPTOMANIA

The second of the spectrum disorders is kleptomania. In this condition, the person is compelled to steal. In a congregational setting, the person about whom one might hear is a young child. Often what is stolen are senseless items, which are thrown away rather than kept. This is not the stealing for personal benefit of the older thief, the "I dare you" of the adolescent, nor is it the "stealing love" or filling loss motivation favored by psychoanalysts. This compulsion is truly strange: it may even break out in a middle-aged Sunday school teacher who finds herself sub-merged in anxiety.

Interestingly, some persons have speculated that St. Augustine might have had some degree of OCD. A passage from *The Confessions of St. Augustine* quite directly hints of kleptomania: "Yet I lusted to thieve and did it compelled by no hunger nor poverty."*

TOURETTE'S SYNDROME

A third condition is Tourette's syndrome. Usually breaking out in late childhood, there are grunts and perhaps barks, usually facial tics and shoulder shrugs and, too frequently, blasphemous utterances of which the sufferer is totally unaware.

Once again we can only remind ourselves that it is pointless to be judgmental. The "filth" is blown out from some level below awareness, with the person most often unable to recall the outburst.

BODY DYSMORPHORIC DISORDER

In body dysmorphoric disorder, the person sees a body feature in a distorted way and consequently hates a part of his or her body; descriptions of the experience sound as if the person is looking into a fun-house mirror.

Many times the person suffering from this disorder is said to be "trapped in a mirror," in that the person will stare endlessly at one of his or her features, fantasizing that others are sickened by the sight of it. As a variant of this, a reader may recall Nathaniel Hawthorne's short story "The Birthmark," in which a husband becomes obsessed about a spot on his wife's face, with disastrous consequences. Now, as then, too many (inevitably) unsuccessful

*For further reading, see Jon E. Grant and S. W. Kim, *Stop Me Because I Can't Stop Myself: Taking Control of Impulsive Behavior.* New York: McGraw-Hill, 2003.

plastic surgeries result, for what surgeon can cut and stitch a malignant perception?*

HYPOCHONDRIASIS

This category of spectrum disorders deserves special consideration by those who visit the sick, even though they may not be knowingly asked, to visit persons with this particular illness. Formerly, someone with hypochondriasis was called a "hypochondriac." One woman in our group suffering from it went to the Internet, but the only information she found was roughly 500 putdown jokes—very roughly, with references to the sufferers as "crocks."

The person suffering from hypochondriasis is not living a bad joke. The physical condition revolving around anxiety has to do with the exaggeration of a physical sensation; it amounts to a reflex thought in OCD terms. The person then begins to obsess about the sensation, typically consulting medical dictionaries, next going to this or that doctor and from there to yet another specialist, from this test to that more refined test, always forced to try to get an explanation of a physical sensation that almost everyone else is able to dismiss. Usually doctors recognize it as an exaggeration of the normal, provide that explanation, and hope to let the matter drop.

In the best-case scenario, the sufferer lets it drop, too—until the next sensation insinuates it is beyond the normal. Then the doubting disease's interpretation of a serious illness begins to churn. The questioning begins whether it is really "nothing," and spouses and friends start repeating reassurances. Still the ritual begins: off to the books and articles, off to the doctors, try this test/that test. It gobbles the hours and the days and raises the need to find a place to store all the aging insurance forms.**

---

*For further reading, see Katharine A. Phillips, *The Broken Mirror: Understanding and Treating Body Dysmorphic Disorder.* New York: Oxford University Press, 1996.

**Carla Cantor, with Brian A. Fallon, *Phantom Illness: Shattering the Myth of Hypochondria.* Boston: Houghton Mifflin Co., 1996.

SUMMARY

The lesson to be learned from these conditions is not that those in pastoral care should develop an interest in abnormal psychology. It is rather that angst can compel persons to respond in strange and dangerous ways, and the person in pastoral care should have expertise in sensing heavy-duty anxiety. Inviting appropriate sharing should be followed by a referral. As an outcome, both psychotherapist and pastoral caregivers ought to welcome collaboration as the person in pastoral care helps a sufferer to move from wayward areas of dread into courageous growth.

Index